THE SURPRISE FACTOR

Gospel Strategies for Changing
the Game at Your Church

KIM SHOCKLEY
PAUL NIXON

Abingdon Press
Nashville

THE SURPRISE FACTOR
GOSPEL STRATEGIES FOR CHANGING THE GAME AT YOUR CHURCH

Copyright © 2012 by Abingdon Press

All rights reserved.

This book is printed on acid-free paper.

Library of Congress Cataloging-in-Publication Data has been requested.

ISBN 978-1-4267-4239-2

Scripture quotations marked NRSV are taken from the New Revised Standard Version of the Bible, copyright 1989, Division of Christian Education of the National Council of the Churches of Christ in the United States of America. Used by permission. All rights reserved.

Scripture quotations marked CEB are from the Common English Bible. Copyright © 2011 by the Common English Bible. All rights reserved. Used by permission. www.CommonEnglishBible.com.

Scripture quotations marked NIV are taken from the Holy Bible, New International Version®, NIV® Copyright © 1973, 1978, 1984, 2011 by Biblica, Inc.™ Used by permission. All rights reserved worldwide. www.zondervan.com.

Scripture quotations marked *THE MESSAGE* are taken from *THE MESSAGE*. Copyright © by Eugene H. Peterson 1993, 1994, 1995, 1996, 2000, 2001, 2002. Used by permission of NavPress Publishing Group.

Scripture quotations marked NLT are taken from *Holy Bible,* New Living Translation, copyright © 1996. Used by permission of Tyndale House Publishers, Inc., Wheaton, Illinois 60189. All rights reserved.

Except where permission is provided for use of an individual's story or name, all stories of individual persons or groups are representative of our experience and do not refer to specific persons.

12 13 14 15 16 17 18 19 20 21—10 9 8 7 6 5 4 3 2 1

MANUFACTURED IN THE UNITED STATES OF AMERICA

*To Gary—Kim's life partner and one of Paul's dearest friends—
thanks for your good humor, your encouragement, and your patience
through the months of this project!*

CONTENTS

INTRODUCTION

This is a book about leadership strategy.

Specifically, it is about strategies for upending the status quo in your church—in order to usher in a new era of thriving, community-relevant ministry.

Both of us (Kim and Paul) have been studying and writing about effective church leadership for years, but neither of us has written a book focused entirely on leader strategy. Our recent projects have focused on:

- Critical choices that great churches make (*I Refuse to Lead a Dying Church!* [Cleveland: Pilgrim Press, 2006])

- Ways of reimagining church (*Imagining Church: Seeing Hope in a World of Change* [Herndon, Va.: Alban Institute, 2009])

- Church as a spiritual pilgrimage into new social territory (*Finding Jesus on the Metro* [Cleveland: Pilgrim Press, 2009])

- Ways that churches can reconnect with their core identities (*Healing Spiritual Amnesia* [Nashville: Abingdon Press, 2004])

- The multisite congregation (*Fling Open the Doors* [Nashville: Abingdon Press, 2002])

- Ways that churches can multiply their impact for good in the world (*The Readiness 360 Project,* 2011–12, http://readiness360.org/)

In 2011, Paul wrote a book that details fifteen amazing church-turnaround stories, *We Refused to Lead a Dying Church!* During the same time, Kim led one of the most far-reaching studies of church transformation in the history of The United Methodist Church. For every story that Paul shared in his last book, Kim studied half a dozen!

In all of this study, we have discovered two overarching common denominators—the presence and power of the Holy Spirit and good leaders on the ground, who lead strategically and responsively to the unique situation in their churches.

For all we have written, and for most of the literature that abounds in the field of transformational church leadership, this book addresses an oft-missing piece: *the strategy of rallying people and coalescing the beginnings of a movement.* Regardless of your theology or your vision, if you intend to lead a group of people to a very new place, then there are a few critical issues that you must tend to. *Everywhere you find resistance and push back, you must be ready to surprise folks!*

As we studied and unpacked the concept of *strategy,* we learned a few things:

- The concept of strategy arose as a component of war theory.

- A strategy is actually a string of surprise moves against an opponent. We might think of these surprise moves, called *stratagems,* as the building blocks of a strategy.

- Such tricky moves catch an opponent off guard. Depending on the scale of the surprise, the results can range from an opponent merely thrown off-balance to an opponent who loses battlefield advantage to an opponent who quits fighting or surrenders.

- The metaphors of war, opponents, and even kingdoms (or empires) are violent and often troubling. Yet Jesus turns these concepts upside down:

  o Who in the first century ever heard of an empire run like

the kingdom of heaven? It was, in several respects, an un-kingdom. If the empire of Caesar was the yin, then the kingdom of heaven was the yang.

o Jesus, the peaceful warrior, fought for this kingdom using exclusively nonviolent means. He was a master of nonviolent strategy as a movement leader.

• Jesus' strategy playbook is as relevant for leaders of movements today as it was then.

• His strategies are especially relevant for those who seek to lead as change agents within faith communities. (More about this in a moment!)

Regardless of the particular choices or paradigms or signature ministries that will underline a church's journey into new life, their leaders must lead them! And surprise them! Where no surprise factor occurs, you will rarely find a real game-change in the life of a church. The pastoral leader must collect allies systematically and persistently. He or she will meet resistance at various points. In many cases, this resistance will offer an opportunity for both the leader and those who see another way to come together and discern a third way that is better than either the status quo or the leader's early proposals. Often, however, resistance to the change that the leader embodies becomes entrenched, causing people to behave as opponents of the change, and sometimes as opponents of the leader and her allies. This is exactly what happened to Jesus' movement as he tangled with the temple culture early in the first century.

To the consternation of a few of Jesus' disciples, Jesus responded to opposition in unconventional ways—*quirky* is not too strong a word for Jesus' responses in some cases! In each case, his responses puzzled folks and threw both his friends and his opponents a bit off-balance, helping advance his movement!

Plenty of traps were set for Jesus. And then he would usually dance right out of the traps! If you are called to lead a church toward transformation in our time, a few traps will probably be set for you as well!

In this book, we look at ten of Jesus' best strategic moves. We lift them right out of Jesus' ministry playbook and explore what it means to live these strategies in our current contexts, specifically in the early stage of a church transformation. We first identified a handful of common strategies in the lives of effective leaders with whom we had worked. Sometime later we stepped back and realized that each of the strategies was an essential element of Jesus' leadership and that *surprise was the common denominator to each of them.* Then through a careful reading of the Gospels, other surprise strategies came to light.

Church transformation comes in stages. As a point of reference, we define these stages as follows:

- Stage 1—Measuring from the low point, weekly participation (worship and groups—no one counted more than once) grows at least 50 percent higher. Or in cases in which members are still dying (or quitting) faster than new folks are coming in, stage 1 might stretch simply toward the moment at which one half or more of the active participants have come along during the current pastor's tenure. By the end of stage 1, conflict may be rising due to grieving and resistance among some leaders.

- Stage 2—From the end of stage 1 until the "mutiny" is resolved or until weekly participation is 125 percent higher than the low point. By the end of stage 2, new core values are fully integrated into church life and modeled by the leadership team.

- Stage 3—The church is uniting and aligning toward a clear sense of mission, steadily reaching and assimilating new people into its life, modeling healthy relationship at all levels, and morphing constantly in the spirit of Christ and responding to the needs of the wider community.

The majority of attempts at church transformation never make it to stage 2. The strategies that we lay out significantly improve the chances that a church will make it all the way through the transformation process to fully embody a new day.

You may be saying to yourself, "But Jesus got crucified in the end." This is true, and leading change in some systems will provoke responses that intense. Please remember two things on this point: (1) Jesus succeeded as a change agent, and (2) few if any Protestant congregations in North America will kill you if they oppose your leadership. Your family may suffer, and you may get fired. When human beings feel threatened, they can get mean! And transformational leadership is almost inevitably going to threaten some otherwise good folks!

We have approached this book as a conversation. In the ten major chapters, we have kept our voices distinct. Each chapter focuses on a distinct strategy or surprising move. The conversational nature of the chapters is intended to invite you and fellow leaders at your church to join the conversation as you read the book together. A free study guide is available for download at www.epicentergroup.org along with a blog that invites readers to join in this conversation.

In particular, the conversation here is between a layperson and a pastor. We believe that dynamic lay-clergy conversation and collaboration is critical if churches are to experience healthy and lasting change.

Kim is a Christian educator who chose years ago to remain a layperson in church life. In recent years, her work has focused on leadership coaching for local church leadership teams for whom ministry transformation is the goal. For the last two years, she has led a landmark study—Toward Vitality—of what church transformation looks like in all parts of the United States within The United Methodist Church, a study that is sponsored by the denomination.

Paul is an ordained clergyperson who served nineteen years as a pastoral leader in growing congregations. He has coached and consulted with hundreds of Christian leaders. Paul is President/CEO of two organizations: Epicenter Group, a leadership coaching organization working with about 100 churches a year (many of which are new starts), and Readiness 360, a company that offers assessments of local church readiness for risk-taking mission to new groups of people. Paul also serves as a new-church strategist for the Path 1 movement, a nationwide initiative within The United Methodist Church to plant 1,000 new faith communities between 2012 and 2016.

We met each other in 2008. We quickly became friends and trusted colleagues. This is our first book together, and we hope that you are drawn into our conversation. We invite you to weigh in with your thoughts and experiences on our blog: "The Surprise Factor" (see www.epicentergroup.org). And beyond that, we pray the very best for your journey as you seek to lead your congregation, with surprising moves, toward renewed life in a new day!

One

SEEK SIGNIFICANT GOD-ENCOUNTER

KIM: *I grew up in a large congregation in Hummelstown, Pennsylvania. Ours was a healthy, vibrant church and a great place to be a kid! Once the church held some kind of spiritual renewal weekend. One night after all the folks had gone home, both of our pastors (Fred and Jacob) experienced a numinous encounter with God and a revelation about their ministry. Fred and Jacob, each excited over what they believed to be a unique and special message from God, went looking for the other throughout the building. Turning out lights as they went, suddenly they ran into each other in the dark, literally, at the bottom of some steps. Pastor Fred was of medium height, but Pastor Jacob was significantly taller, so he needed to help his colleague off the floor! In sharing what they believed God had told them, they discovered they had each received the same message!*

This happened a long time ago, and I was a teenager, so I don't remember the specific message that came to these guys. But I do remember that it changed the way that they worked together. They became a team, working in union to bring God's dreams to life through our church. Everything was different from that night forward. And it happened because they were both listening and open for God's message for their congregation.

PAUL: *You know, Kim, around a quarter century after Jacob and Fred*

1

crashed into a common vision, something like that happened in the church where I served on the northwest Florida coast. Our church was growing steadily, far beyond what our five-acre campus could sustain. We had been negotiating with the owners of an adjacent acre to pay an astronomical sum to acquire a small addition of land, when suddenly they stopped talking to us. There may have been some personal history between the owners and the man negotiating for us—but whatever the case, the deal was suddenly dead, and the owners swore they would never ever sell to us. It knocked us back, and we felt a wave of terrible discouragement. Yet, once that door was closed, we were freed to think more broadly and to let God show us a better plan.

Two weeks after the purchase fell through, seven of us experienced a Pentecost-style aha moment in a little upstairs room of a waterfront café. It was some of the most exhilarating two hours of my life. One week more and we had purchased thirteen acres for the price we were prepared to pay for the one, eight miles to our east—and the Soundside campus of Gulf Breeze Church was born. The Soundside campus would carry us much further in ministry to our community than anything we could have possibly achieved at the original site.

KIM: We live in an era when many books have been written on ministry principles and church-growth tricks. It is tempting to begin thinking of ministry as a business like any other. Yet this is not just a business. It is a surprising movement of God's Spirit, with the purpose of transforming our world with the love and grace of Jesus Christ!

PAUL: And until we collide with God's Spirit, or we hit the limits of what we can do simply from a human angle—until then, we mostly just tinker around the edges of what is truly possible.

Jesus led a spiritual movement that was world altering in its effect. Can you imagine Jesus effective in leading such a thing without a significant God-encounter? It took thirty years of intense spiritual formation to produce three productive years as a leader.

KIM: Even during those three years, Jesus took significant opportunity to connect with God. It seems to me he was often looking for a chance to escape the crowds and be with his Father.

God made us with a variety of personalities and gifts. God-encounters will look different from one of us to the next. While I crave my alone time with God and Scripture, others crave different pathways to God.

PAUL: And we come from a variety of theological personalities and traditions as well. In my work with the *Readiness 360* congregational inventory (www.readiness360.org) in diverse churches across the United States, people report God-encounters in radically different ways.

KIM: So it should be no surprise that there are many ways that folks experience a living relationship with Christ. I have a friend who literally prays in a dark closet as Jesus suggested, but dark closets don't work for me, except to store things. Others like getting up early to spend time with God, and some folks end the day with God.

PAUL: Some folks pray with great freedom, creativity, and spontaneity. Others depend on structure. Some gather morning and evening as intentional communities to observe a set liturgy together that marks the spiritual rhythm of their days…and they listen for God. Some of our taxi drivers in DC have little rugs rolled up in the trunk, which they roll out five times a day, somewhere alongside the road. To pray.

KIM: There seem to be almost as many ways to pray as there are people in the world. But however we get at it, the disciplines of prayer, meditation, study, Scripture reading, fasting, and even rest, all provide opportunities to run into God.

PAUL:…and for God to crash into us! Annie Dillard is probably over-quoted for her observation that if we really understood the One we were dealing with when we come to worship God, we would all wear crash helmets! (Annie Dillard has said other things I like, but that's like the John 3:16 of Annie Dillard. Find this reference in *Teaching a Stone to Talk* [New York: Perennial Library, 1988], 52.)

KIM: Over the years I've observed a correlation between how much time a group of leaders spends in prayer and how effective their congregation is in reaching new people and providing vital ministry to their community. Praying congregations realize they can offer a redemptive presence in a place only when they stay connected to their Redeemer.

PAUL: I hear that, and I agree with it—and yet I know that some of the folks who read this will assume that we are talking about only very pietistic churches. I think we have to doubly underline your earlier point that prayer-fulness looks different in each place. Spiritual discernment and watchfulness look different in a Louisiana Pentecostal church on the one hand and a New England Episcopal church on the other. But there can be spiritual collision in either place.

KIM: Definitely! One clue as to the spiritual grounding of almost any faith community—left, right, urban, or rural—is the relative absence of fear. The opposite of living in a vital relationship with Christ is living in fear. When I hear fear expressed as the first emotion in a change situation, I pay close attention. We are afraid of hurting someone's feelings, we are afraid of financial situations, or we are afraid that someone will leave our church or that the "wrong" people will start attending. We are afraid that we will do the wrong thing or fail doing the right thing. We are afraid that we will upset the power people or the money people...the list goes on and on. Fear is normal, but when it takes over, it is a sign that we need to get recentered spiritually as a community.

PAUL: When churches or families or nations act out of fear, they often move in ways contrary to the Spirit of God. Sometimes they can't even recognize the surprising ways that God acts because they are clouded by fear. When we truly and fully abide in Christ, fear somehow gets cast out.

KIM: What do we really have to fear? "If God is for us, who can be against us?" (Rom. 8:31 NIV). God says, "I will be with you!" to Abraham, Jacob, Moses, and Joshua over and over again—a promise of God to God's people throughout the Scriptures!

PAUL: Fear can really mess with our minds, when we dwell in it. As a person who lives in downtown Washington DC, I have observed how special-interest groups use fear to manipulate voters and elected officials in ways that pull at the very seams of our collective covenant as a nation.

And then we go to church, many of us already reeling from changes and crisis in our families and in the larger society. It is very tempting and easy to turn our church into a Monument to Fear: a fortress against all that is out there, a place to cower, and a place from which we can vainly seek to freeze the world on its axis. Some of the worst fights I have seen at church are related to human attempts to try to freeze changes that scare us. In a world changing so profoundly, a lot of people would do almost anything to preserve their churches as bastions of comfort and peace set apart from a world in flux.

KIM: I've seen this too. We try to prepare for the future by looking backward—seeking comfort in recalling what we have done successfully in the past.

PAUL: Or sometimes reimagining how wonderful things were in the past. Or recalling a time when we felt more in control of things!

KIM: I do find it interesting, as one pastor pointed out to me, that many of the folks who want the church to look backward are getting text messages from their grandchildren on their iPhones!

PAUL: Yes, and taking full advantage of the latest medical technology to manage their health . . . so most of us definitely are receptive to some change. I think we are more apt to fear and resist change when it affects our sense of control.

The greatest God-encounter that I can think of in history was the original Pentecost event. Before the Spirit came and knocked them sideways, Luke tells us that Jesus' remnant band of disciples were cowering together behind locked doors. The events in the preceding days had spun utterly out of control. They were afraid of what might happen next! Afraid of the authorities! Afraid of the world! Not sure what to do next. Before the Spirit of God descended on that room and kick-started this movement that we call the church, the people of God were twisted into a spiritual fetal position.

Several years ago, I found myself on a strange church mission trip in Russia. Through a sequence of events, we came to believe that our mission team had accidentally run afoul of the Russian mafia because they believed someone in our group had seen and heard something we were not supposed to know about. Then a strange tourist appeared with a camera to take our photo in twenty-below-zero weather because he said he had never seen Americans before . . . or maybe the photos were for the hit men. A pit settled in my stomach, and paranoia arose that I was going to die in Russia. It was not rational at all, but it was very real. I felt robbed of any control in the situation. I remember going back to the room where I was lodging (at a former KGB retreat center), and I was so angry with God.

When finally I boarded the Delta jet in Saint Petersburg to get out of there, I wanted to bend down and kiss the aisle. And then on the ride home, somewhere over the Atlantic Ocean, I began to feel silly about the whole episode. I realized that I had more in common with the Apostle Peter on Holy

Thursday than I ever knew. When I was twenty years old, I don't think the danger would have fazed me so much, but by the time of the trip, I had a young child and a promising career. I felt like I had more to lose.

The Russia incident was a wake-up call to me that I had lost some of my spiritual focus. This happens to churches and church leaders all the time!

KIM: Definitely. Fear colors how we think about everything! That was certainly your experience in Russia!

While fear can be one clue to a congregation's overall health, another clue is how the people experience God's call, both individually and as a group.

PAUL: I see that. One of the marks of healthy churches is that individuals are regularly experiencing the call of God to varied kinds of ministries and endeavors—and then responding to that call by teaming together to bring to pass the visions that God has planted in their collective imagination.

But too often, in even relatively healthy churches, the whole issue of God's call is understood too narrowly, associated with the personal journey into ordained ministry or into a ministry-related career. Don't you think that misses the point?

KIM: Geez, Paul. *Misses the point* would be putting it lightly.

Too often, we laypeople have willingly given up the sense of being called as something meant exclusively for the professionals. And, Paul, all you clergy-professionals have willingly taken the mantle of God's call and worn it proudly. Dr. Jeff Stiggins, executive director of the Center for Congregational Excellence in the Florida Conference of The United Methodist Church, writes that the call of laity to ministry has been ignored since the Middle Ages:

> The professionalization of ministry has made matters even worse, if that was possible. Many people...assume that ministry belongs exclusively to those few special persons called, educated and ordained as professional ministers. It is the lot of laity to be appreciative recipients of their ministry or, at most, to play supportive roles to the ministry of the ordained. Consequently, most clergy are exhausted trying to do the ministry of the whole Body of Christ and most laity are underutilized in the mission of Christ in the world. (http://floridaconferenceconnection.info/blogs/detail/187)

One way this may be played out in congregations is when the phrase "that's what we hired the pastor to do" is heard coming from lay folks! So, I would like to provide another way to think of God's calling that can apply to everyone. *A call is a sense of how God invites and empowers me to have impact for God's kingdom through my life.*

PAUL: In the years when I worked as a church development director for my bishop, I found myself in a different church almost every Sunday. There was a strong Emmaus movement in our region. Some churches had sent a whole generation of their lay leadership on Walks to Emmaus. Others had not. It got to where I could walk into a church community on a Sunday morning and tell in about ten minutes if a few people in that place had been to Emmaus or not. The Emmaus churches had made spiritual development a priority, and they were usually miles ahead of other churches in their warmth and hospitality to me, the stranger. The Emmaus churches typically had a group of folks who had discovered their own spiritual gifts and call, and they were living this out. So I experienced a more functional and winsome group of people in my Sunday encounter.

KIM: I've never participated in an Emmaus weekend. In fact, I've been in places where the Emmaus folks get cliquish and inwardly focused, and others like the ones you describe, Paul. There are lots of ways that people can get connected to their callings!

PAUL: No doubt what I observed had to do with the health of the Emmaus community in our area and the way it fit folks theologically and culturally in that region.

There are many churches that cultivate God-encounter in the lives of their people without hauling people up the mountain in a van to a retreat center. In almost every case of this, however, some person or group in the church is working intentionally, inviting people to places of likely God-encounter, where they can rethink their lives in terms of the story that God intends to write through them. One of the time-proven methods for setting up a church for significant God-encounter is to invite folks to study through the New Testament book of Acts. (A wonderful resource for leading a church to rethink its life through the Acts lens is a resource titled *Catch Fire in Fifty Days*, created by a group of laity and clergy in northern California and Nevada.)

KIM: I visited with a church last week that does something they call Encounter Weekend—more than 1,600 people have experienced this in the past ten years. Needless to say, they have one of the most empowered and called congregations that I have experienced!

PAUL: If I can go back to the story you told at the beginning of this chapter, I am still pondering the crash imagery of Jacob and Fred in the church hallway. The call of God does often come with impact, even injury.

The biblical story of Jacob comes to mind: wrestling all night with God's angel for a blessing. Jacob got his blessing. Alongside the promise of God's blessing for himself and his descendants, however, he received a call to serve God and others. The blessing and the call came as a package deal. Theologically, they cannot be separated. And as testimony to the rough-and-tumble nature of that all-night encounter, Jacob walked away from his experience of call with a limp. He was permanently wounded by the impact, so that he would never be able to get out of bed or walk across a room again without immediately remembering the night by the River Jabbok, where he wrestled with God and lived to tell about it. Some folks hang ordination certificates on the wall as a sort of souvenir of their call. Jacob's souvenir was a bad hip.

KIM: And, as I recall the story, Jacob was afraid and on the run when his God-encounter came, too.

PAUL: That's right.

KIM: A big part of my call is to remind church people that they have a purpose to live a winsome life that attracts folks to the gospel. So in essence, my impact is multiplied when they can act out the gospel in their own lives! We all carry scars and limps that come from significant parts of our living. Sometimes we just don't see them as the ways that God molds us and prepares us to be in mission and ministry; they are just "life." What an eye-opening and life-changing thing it would be to see God's hand in those experiences.

PAUL: Wow! I think you have just pinpointed something important in my experience of call; each aspect of my own call is related to some kind of struggle or injury in my life. God made each of the scars and limps holy; and today they cumulatively define the best of what I am and what God is leading me to be. It casts light on the mystery of why God refused to remove the Apostle Paul's "thorn…in the flesh" (see 2 Cor. 12:7 NRSV). Without it, perhaps he would have been just another grumpy, talk-radio guy. With it, God used him to change the world in a wonderful way.

KIM: My siblings and I lost our parents to cancer within a year and a half of each other—Mom was fifty-nine years old, and Dad was sixty-one. It would have been very easy for me to rail at God and become bitter and lost in that grief. Instead I turned to God as the Comforter, and in the passing years I can see how that time in my life made it more possible for me to understand the grief of others. It gave me a softer side toward people that I just didn't have before and a story to share that has a positive impact on God's kingdom.

PAUL: The Great Commission (Go make disciples! see Matthew 28) and the Great Commandment (Love God and neighbor! see Luke 10:25-28) must be taken together if we are to begin to wrap our minds around God's purposes and dreams for us. The Great Commission calls us to a grand idea and invites us to call others to it. But James says faith ideas without an action agenda are dead, useless (see James 2)! The Great Commandment is about putting love and faith into action. Love without theological grounding can get very shallow very fast and can exhaust us in the process.

Yet taken together, these two missional foci work as sort of a yin and yang, and they begin to capture the genius of the Christian faith.

KIM: It always fascinates me how congregations can latch on to one of these "Greats" but not both. I've been in churches where the emphasis is saving souls, and they do this well. People come to the altar and receive Jesus as Savior, hang around for a few weeks, and then wander back to their old lives.

Other churches do a wonderful job of meeting the needs of their communities; they feed people, clothe people, visit people, tutor people, and teach people English, but they forget to build relationships with these people so that they can share the wonderful story of God's love for them through Jesus.

In order to experience God's call, as we have defined it, we have to recognize both the Great Commandment and the Great Commission for ourselves. They simply go together. How can I love God and my neighbor and not want others to have what I have received through relationship with Christ?

PAUL: You and I have coached churches that err in both directions. The most effective churches always seem to find a sweet spot in which they integrate the call to share a message and the call to love into a single vision. And, honestly, what else is a disciple, but a person who is apprenticing with Jesus to learn more perfectly how to love God and neighbor?

But back to your point about spiritual grounding. Obviously, it is helpful if the pastor is living out an authentic call to ministry. But I hear you suggesting that a good number of the church members should be doing this also if a church is to have significant spiritual foundations.

KIM: Yes. One of the men from our last congregation got connected with an outreach program that brings weekend worship and learning experiences to incarcerated men and women. Gus is struggling with this as a sense of calling, even to the point of wondering if it will lead him into more professional ministry opportunities. What a great time of exploration for him as he learns how God has empowered him to make a difference in God's kingdom! I celebrate this experience for him—his love for God overflows and touches other people's lives. Can it get any better than this?

PAUL: When you know that you are living out God's purposes and utilizing the gifts God has given you to bless others, that's as good as it gets.

So, is there a good way to think about how our attitudes, actions, and behaviors as individuals can impact who we are as congregations?

KIM: There is! God-encounter, for both individuals and congregations, is also countercultural, even counterintuitive—just like the gospel! In his writing "Four Postures of Spiritual Authority," Gary R. Mays defines "spiritual authority" as

> that quality found in leaders who speak with an authority beyond themselves. It is what some might call God's anointing. It comes from the unmistakable presence of God in a person's life. It is the fragrance of Jesus. It is what those who heard Jesus teach experienced when they "were amazed at his teaching, because he taught as one who had authority, and not as their teachers of the law" (Matt. 7:28-29).

Mays defines the postures (the way it is acted out) of spiritual authority as

- Surrender—putting God in control;

- Alignment—learning to use God's ideas and plans;

- Brokenness—recognizing that God is the expert;

- Vulnerability—having full dependence on God.

(http://www.issuu.com/noredcapes/docs/nrc_four_postures_of_ spiritual_authority, July 2012)

PAUL: In those last two postures, I again see the connection between our wounds and limps and the dynamic edge of what God does with us as leaders.

KIM: Definitely! Most often we think of authority as that which comes from other kinds of sources: because I'm the boss, because I'm the expert, or because you've learned to trust our relationship (I'm the Mom, that's why!).

PAUL: The term *authority* can feel coercive or pushy, at least the way we often use it. Yet Jesus refrained from coerciveness. He held his ground on certain matters, but he did not force people to follow him. People followed him because they respected him. That's spiritual authority. And obviously, as Mays observes, spiritual authority happens because we live with appropriate postures toward God.

KIM: I see spiritual authority as the attitude that will help us develop into people who are open and willing to be used by God to have the kind of impact that will cause God's will to be done on earth as it is in heaven. When we realize that it is not about me, but about how God uses me, then we can be congregations full of light and salt and pleasing fragrances to God!

PAUL: It is hard even to scratch the surface of what it means for a congregation to mature spiritually in just a few pages!

KIM: We should remind people that we have included a list of ideas and resources for each of the ten strategies in this book in the free downloadable study guide that accompanies this book (available at www.epicentergroup).

PAUL: In this chapter's conversation, we have hit on a few key ideas that folks may wish to explore further. The study guide will help folks to do just that. We have suggested here that:

- God-encounters can knock us down. There may be an almost traumatic quality to such events, and these encounters can be both individual and corporate.

- Similarly, other high-impact and wounding life experiences—*not from God*—also may knock us down. God's surprise factor may be, rather, to redeem these bad experiences and weave them into our life's call.

- All sorts of human beings—both laity and clergy—may experience a sense of call in response to encounter with God.

- When a church lives with a high awareness of God-encounters, fear no longer dominates, and a strong sense of mission and purpose emerges.

- There is great variety to both the spiritual practices undergirding God-encounters and the form of the encounters because people are so varied.

- Our response to God's encounters with us ultimately may be judged in terms of how well we follow the Spirit and the contours of the Great Commission and the Great Commandment.

KIM: And you know, even when we are looking for it, working for it, praying and longing for it for years, a God-encounter always feels like a surprise!

PAUL: Totally. These kinds of events come like electroshock, able to change anything and everything in a moment.

And Jesus knew this better than anyone.

Now Jesus, full of the Holy Spirit, left the Jordan and was led by the Spirit into the wild.... (Luke 4:1 *THE MESSAGE*)

While it was still night, way before dawn, he got up and went out to a secluded spot and prayed.... (Mark 1:35 *THE MESSAGE*)

In the course of their meal, having taken and blessed the bread, he broke it and gave it to them. Then he said, "Take, this is my body." Taking the chalice, he gave it to them, thanking God, and they all drank from it. He said, "This is my blood, God's new covenant, Poured out for many people." (Mark 14:22-24 *THE MESSAGE*)

Then Jesus went with them to a garden called Gethsemane and told his disciples, "Stay here while I go over there and pray." Taking along Peter and the two sons of Zebedee, he plunged into an agonizing sorrow. Then he said, "This sorrow is crushing my life out. Stay here and keep vigil with me."

Going a little ahead, he fell on his face, praying, "My Father, if there is any way, get me out of this. But please, not what I want. You, what do *you* want?"

When he came back to his disciples, he found them sound asleep. He said to Peter, "Can't you stick it out with me a single hour? Stay alert; be in prayer so you don't wander into temptation without even knowing you're in danger. There is a part of you that is eager, ready for anything in God. But there's another part that's as lazy as an old dog sleeping by the fire." (Matthew 26:36-41 *THE MESSAGE*)

Two

LOVE ONE ANOTHER

Bart has been pastor of Maplewood Church for about a year. The preceding pastor, during her Maplewood years, moved steadily off Maplewood's map theologically, until she was perceived as a radical and a maverick—both within and beyond the congregation. One day, she quit in frustration—to the relief of all. A few months later, Bart came along—with the widely shared hope that Maplewood could rediscover its balance and begin to have some fun again.

Maplewood faces an uphill road. The Maplewood folks are significantly older than their surrounding community, significantly more white, significantly more affluent, significantly more into classical music, and significantly disconnected from the immediate neighborhood around the church. Where once Maplewood's members lived near the church, now they commute on Sundays from homes scattered across a two-county area.

When Bart first arrived, he heard lots of talk about the need to attract younger people, to "build Maplewood back," and, of course, to reclaim the theological middle ground that his predecessor had abandoned.

The first few months have seen a slight uptick in worship attendance and a good Christmas cantata. But the congregation remains socially isolated and seems stuck in its ability to adapt to its surrounding community. A couple of folks at Maplewood see their role to be the church "Tea Partiers," doing all they can to keep the church from spending money. They delight in the political metaphor. At a recent church council meeting, one of the Tea Partiers went into a rant, directed largely at Bart. After the meeting, Bart was so traumatized that he could not fully recall what the rant had been about. All Bart could think was this: "I came here to love these people and help their church grow. What have I done to deserve this?"

Plenty of pastors would have begun packing their bags after an outburst in a council meeting, emotionally if not literally. But Bart has chosen to look past the bad meeting and past the challenges that loom ever larger, to focus on the dear friends he has made within the Maplewood parish over the past year. He realizes that nothing positive will come from his fleeing or from allowing a couple of bullies to disrupt God's dreams for Maplewood.

So Bart has set himself apart from the pack. He chose, at the very moment he was attacked, to love the people of Maplewood more intentionally than ever. He has looked deep within his soul and reconfirmed that God has lovingly called him here, more profoundly than any external machination of church polity. From that awareness, a sense of compassion for his people continues to bubble up.

And with Bart's decision to love Maplewood more—at the moment when they become harder to love—Maplewood moves one step closer to transformation and renewal.

PAUL: We have all known pastors with grand plans to transform their churches, pastors with big heady ideas. Often they fail to get anywhere, and one key reason is that they fail to fall in love with the folks they are called to serve.

It is easier to fall in love with a romantic caricature of the church we serve—for example, to fall in love with the reputation that the church had in the 1960s within the denomination. Or, just like new lovers bitten with infatuation, a pastor and people can fall in love with caricatures of one another—based on seeing only what we desire to see. In other cases, I see pastors with great leader potential who take the opposite track and view the pastoral relationship as a political chess game in which the people who disagree with them are quickly labeled controllers or enemies whom they must outfox and defeat. Neither the honeymoon nor the holy-war paradigm is helpful.

It is common to find one or two folks in a church leadership mix who intimidate the rest of the leaders and whose overall impact on the church is negative. You may indeed have to outfox these characters at some point. In the meantime, I advocate praying for them daily—especially in the months or years when you are stuck with them, and they are still empowered within the congregation's leadership system. You may just be amazed that praying for them changes both you and them! Further, as you look beyond a few negative souls, you will often discover many, many others who long for loving relationships in their church, and who are ready to embrace a loving relationship with their pastor.

Kim, have you ever seen a pastor lead a successful transformation process when she or he did not love her or his church, warts and all?

KIM: No, I have not. I have seen a few who loved their congregations to the best of their ability and still could not bring lasting transformation, so it certainly isn't a guarantee of change. I would say, though, without loving the people there's no chance of true transformation.

PAUL: I have seen a few coups in which a host of new people flood an old church and basically take over the place without the hard work of forging partnerships with the existing leaders of that church, and that can be an effective strategy for changing a church's direction. But unless you have a host of new folks massed on the sidelines, there is no dependable road to church transformation without love. And love is never an easy thing.

Kim, you and (your husband) Gary ran into one or two tough churches over the years. How did you guys learn to love people when they are afraid of the future—and sometimes afraid of you—and are obstinate and defensive?

KIM: Our first assignment after seminary was to a village in north central Pennsylvania where Gary was to serve three congregations scattered through the southern part of the county. This place was so different from any other place I had lived, that it took me two or three years to begin to learn how to love the people. Gary figured it out immediately, so I followed his lead in learning to love. When we arrived, the largest of the three churches had the most potential for transformation, but they also had the most difficult personalities in leadership. I can honestly say that we both had to make daily decisions to love no matter what. We turned to the Gospels for our coaching.

Jesus oozed love! It wasn't a mushy kind of love, but a more realistic love that had expectations and accountability along with deep caring and encouragement. When Jesus called Simon and Andrew and James and John, he simply said, "Come, follow me, and I will show you how to fish for people!"

(Matt. 4:19 NLT). They had a brief window of opportunity to follow Jesus; I'm not sure that Jesus would have come back to beg them.

PAUL: When I think about Jesus and his team, I find it amazing that he never fired any of them. Even when Judas derailed, Jesus never fired him from discipleship. There is ample evidence that the disciples struggled to *get it* throughout the time that Jesus mentored them. They were constantly on a different page, thinking in different paradigms from their leader. But no one got fired once they were in Jesus' faith community.

Whether you as leader pick your starting lineup, or you inherit a team that has been around a while, each leader ultimately will add some folks to the existing team. And you will rotate some folks off leadership—who will usually remain a part of the church and a part of the beloved community. Meanwhile, team additions can prove to be pivotal in your church's transformation.

Yet all of these people are human beings, prone to wander, prone to misunderstand, prone to hurt feelings, and prone to substitute their own personal agendas for God's.

KIM: Jesus was always willing to give folks another chance, but he never watered down the expectations of team members. In that Pennsylvania congregation, one particular church leader really struggled with the change that was happening. In some ways, she tried to sabotage the change, and it was necessary to help her see her own actions in the light of the mission and ministry of that church. Eventually, after multiple patient meetings, Gary helped her see the broader vision of God's activity in their community.

PAUL: He helped her get clear about where the church was headed. Clarity of expectations from leadership is always a gift to the team. Not once do we have a recorded instance of Jesus watering down the ideals of his movement to accommodate people with half-hearted commitment. Grace, yes! Patience, yes! Casual faith, not a chance!

KIM: The Sermon on the Mount, in Matthew 5–7, gives us a good look at Jesus' playbook around the strategy of loving difficult people and also around his expectations of his followers. Have you read it lately?

PAUL: Actually, I came to my first experience of faith in Christ through an encounter with those rigorous three chapters of Jesus' teaching. It was at summer camp in the San Jacinto Mountains of Southern California. A nerdy guy read us the Sermon on the Mount a little bit each morning, under a pine tree, and it captured me. If it had been easy stuff, I probably would have daydreamed through that week and missed the greatest gift of my life! Jesus captured my young imagination precisely because he was a radical, and he asked so much of me!

KIM: "Turn the other cheek." "Love your enemies." "Store your treasures in heaven." "Don't worry." "Stop judging others." This is hard stuff.

PAUL: Very hard stuff. I have struggled with the challenges of Christ's Way all my life, and perhaps Jesus should have fired me years ago, but he has hasn't given up on me yet.

KIM: If Jesus had given up on any of his first disciples, surely Peter would have been high on the list of people who simply flunked out.

PAUL: I sense that Jesus liked Peter as a human being; they had friendship. They probably laughed together over drinks in the evenings. Perhaps good relationship history made Peter a bit easier to love in the hard times.

KIM: My favorite scripture from the Gospel of John, chapter 21, offers us a glimpse at how Jesus truly loved his leaders. He meets up with Peter after his resurrection on the shores of the Sea of Galilee. Jesus knows that Peter denied knowing him and that Peter has now left the movement and gone back to his former work. But Jesus comes to Peter anyway:

> After breakfast Jesus asked Simon Peter, "Simon son of John, do you love me more than these?" "Yes, Lord," Peter replied, "you know I love you." "Then feed my lambs," Jesus told him. Jesus repeated the question: "Simon son of John, do you love me?" "Yes, Lord," Peter said, "you know I love you." "Then take care of my sheep," Jesus said. A third time he asked him, "Simon son of John, do you love me?" Peter was hurt that Jesus asked the question a third time. He said, "Lord, you know everything. You know that I love you." Jesus said, "Then feed my sheep." (John 21:15-17 NLT)

Jesus offered Peter forgiveness, a second chance, and deep love. But he also challenged him and held him accountable to his actions.

PAUL: Such love does not come casually for any of us. But praying for the tough-to-love folks is very helpful. The toughest character God ever called me to love was a guy, back when I was in college, who physically attacked me one day because he did not like my dog. I despised him. His apartment was just behind where I lived. Early every morning, I would listen (in bed) as he tried to start his car. It had a bad ignition or a weak battery and took forever to start up. I couldn't bring myself to pray for him, because I was so offended by his overbearing behavior. So I started praying for his car . . . that it would start, and I could go back to sleep. And pretty soon, I began to realize that his life was not any easier than mine. It occurred to me that I had a better automobile. Slowly the poison that I felt toward him evaporated. This was a great lesson to learn at the age of twenty—that when I pray for the difficult people in my life, God does something in me that creates a greater empathy and patience toward them.

Dean Snyder, one of my pastor friends in DC, finds a great lesson in the relationship of the Bible character Daniel to the Babylonian king Nebuchadnezzar. Dean points out that Daniel loved Nebuchadnezzar, with a love based in realism *and* with boundaries. Daniel would never bow down to Nebuchadnezzar's idols. Dean raises the question, "How do you love the church as a pastor, when you see the shortfalls of institutional religion even more than the general public?" How do you love a church that is still a little bit racist and sexist and more than a little bit homophobic, and also love the people whom the church has sinned against? The way to find integrity as a pastor serving an imperfect church is to love the church the way Daniel loved the king he served and the way Jesus loved his disciples: love with eyes wide open, seeing both the shortfalls and the good possibilities for growth and healing. Love, while refusing to bow down to the local idols.*

I find this perspective really helpful in my life.

KIM: Thanks for that reminder, Paul! Love with your eyes wide open— that will preach!

First Corinthians 13:4-7 is familiar to everyone from wedding ceremonies, and it is also an eyes-wide-open love.

> Love is patient and kind. Love is not jealous or boastful or proud or rude. It does not demand it own way. It is not irritable, and it keeps no

---

*Thanks to Dean for permission to use the illustration.

record of being wronged. It does not rejoice about injustice but rejoices whenever the truth wins out. Love never gives up, never loses faith, is always hopeful, and endures through every circumstance. (NLT)

Do you think it's really possible to live 1 Corinthians 13 toward the people we seek to lead and with whom we are church?

PAUL: I think that with God's help we are capable of far more than we might think.

Some folks would consider that biblical passage to be a recipe for wimpiness. But that last line about bold persistence is anything but wimpy.

KIM: One could read this passage and come away feeling that leaders have to give in to every whim of an unhappy church member. So how do we combine the high expectations of Jesus' teaching and 1 Corinthians 13–style love for the sake of our congregations? I think the answer lies in how pastors use their relationships with God to empower how they work with leaders.

PAUL: Back to the first surprise factor—God moves first! We just can't do this on our own.

KIM: Yes. Finally, we can love others well only as our own relationship with God is so full that it spills over onto the people around us. Then we can love fully by living into both the accountability and expectations of Jesus and the "love passage" from 1 Corinthians.

PAUL: But when our lives are not giving credence to our words—when we are not aligning our words and deeds as leaders—we become just noise.

KIM: Clanging symbols.

PAUL: Sometimes we should talk less and live more. A spiritual director once said to me, "Don't bore them with the recipe all day and all night. Just serve them the pie." Live it.

KIM: Saint Francis would add, "And when necessary use words."

PAUL: I suspect that words are necessary more often than we might think. But such words should point away from ourselves—words like "Thank you"; "I appreciate what you said the other night"; "I am so glad that you are along for this journey!"; or "We may not always agree, but you do often help me look at things with a 360 perspective, and I value that." They are not egotistical words, but simple loving words.

KIM: In fifteen years of working with pastors, I have experienced the great variety of men and women whom God calls to local church ministry. Many of them practice love for God's people, especially leaders, and lead congregations to new places of fruitful ministry. The humility of this kind of pastor is noticeable—you can see it in their eyes—their overwhelming desire to be Jesus' hands and feet in a hurting world, yet grounded by the realities of being in the world but not of it (see John 17:14-15 and Rom. 12:2). These are genuine, realistic, hopeful people who truly do let something from beyond them flow out to the people around them.

One pastor that I coached was, in turn, able to use a coaching relationship with his staff. He became the patient listener, encourager, accountability partner, and asker of good questions as a way to empower his staff. His love for them spilled out of him and onto them in visible ways. This certainly didn't mean that everything became peaches and cream for this working team. But because their leader showed love for them in tangible ways, they were all able to work more effectively together. They knew the expectations and were held accountable to them in loving ways.

The opposite kind of pastor is also out there—one who speaks with a lot of "me" language.

PAUL: Wah wah wah wah (to quote Charlie Brown's schoolteacher)!

KIM: "I want this. . . . I did this. . . . What about me? Come see what I'm doing. . . . I want to do it my way. . . . "

PAUL: Sounds more like Nebuchadnezzar talking than Daniel.

KIM: Now, there are times when we all need someone to stand up and give clear direction. But we should be careful about overplaying this kind of leadership, which so easily can settle on one person's ego rather than collaborating with a team and focusing on the mission.

PAUL: It is hard to love people when you are focused on receiving personal attention and accolades.

KIM: Another issue that can get in the way of pastors loving their leaders is the attempt to love everybody single-handedly. In my observation, one pastor can effectively minister to thirty to fifty people. It is not surprising that many churches across the country are close to this size, since so many churches live with the expectation that the pastor will care for everyone in the church.

PAUL: Are you suggesting that I can't love every member of my church equally?

KIM: Well, I suppose you could try, but if your church is large at all, what you have to dole out will be *quite thin*!

PAUL: Then it would be a good idea for pastors to figure out who is their primary flock within the larger church and community. In many cases, most of these persons will be leaders: those who presently lead and those in whom we see good potential to lead. These folks, in turn, can shepherd others. Or they oversee a church system that provides shepherding for many. So, the question becomes, "Who are the forty folks that should form the heart of the leadership team?" And within the forty, who are the key eight, ten, or twelve who can make strategic decisions with the pastor to create the conditions within which great ministry can happen?

KIM: If the pastor is a significant caregiver to key leaders within a congregation, then that pastor is setting an example of how those leaders should love other leaders of the teams, groups, and committees that exist throughout the church system. The loving of these leaders then will spill out onto small groups, Sunday school classes, children's groups, youth groups, and every other imaginable way that people gather within the life of a congregation. This may be the best example of a pyramid scheme!

PAUL: Most pyramid schemes eventually run out of juice and collapse. But this one runs on Holy Spirit.

My friend (and now United Methodist bishop) Young Jin Cho grew a church in my community from under 100 to well over 1,000 in worship, praying each morning through the church directory from A–Z, a few names a day. That is a wonderful thing. But he did not try to provide direct relational caring equally to the more than 1,500 people connected to the church. That would have been impossible! Had Young Jin attempted to function as primary caregiver, the church would have stopped growing when he reached his personal capacity for people-juggling. Wisely, he focused his energy on leading and loving leaders, and he created an atmosphere of prayerful caring.*

KIM: Here are a few questions for a pastor to consider regarding the congregation's leaders:

---

*Thanks to Bishop Cho for the use of his story.

- How do I pray for key leaders?

- How is this different from the way I pray for others within the congregation and community?

- How do I make myself available to key leaders?

- What training opportunities are available for key leaders?

- How are we multiplying leaders for the future?

- How do I show appreciation for the mostly volunteer actions of key leaders?

- Which leaders will I intentionally graduate this year from my direct caregiving and mentoring, so that I can invest deeply in some new leaders?

PAUL: And here are a few questions for laity on the leadership team to consider.

- Is my primary motive in serving on the leadership team to help my church reach for the stars or to receive special attention from others, including the pastor?

- How will I feel when the pastor spends less attention on me and moves on to focus on the next generation of leaders who need to be mentored spiritually?

- How are my colleagues in leadership and I working intentionally to love others and to empower others for ministry?

- How do I pray for my pastor?

- How do I seek to encourage my pastor and his or her family and to show them love?

- How can I and others on our team constructively tell our pastor the truth in love when we see aspects of an issue from a vantage point that our pastor may not have?

- What training opportunities are available for our church's leaders?

- How are we multiplying leaders for our church's future?

- How do we show appreciation for the volunteers who lead the frontline ministry efforts of our church?

KIM: Pastors, what if you practiced investing in the lives of five leaders over the next twelve months? Each month set up a thirty- to sixty-minute coaching time with each one, using the following questions as a guide for your conversation:

- How are you?

- What are you celebrating?

- What challenges are you facing?

- How will you tackle those challenges?

- How can I help you?

- How can I pray for you?

(Dave Ferguson and Jon Ferguson, *Exponential: How You and Your Friends Can Start a Missional Church Movement* [Grand Rapids, MI: Zondervan, 2010], 128)

Here's another thought: what if you encouraged leaders to identify an apprentice leader who would work with them during the next twelve months? Leaders could work closely with the apprentices to teach them their responsibilities and give them opportunities to test their leadership in a supervised way. And, if possible, the pastor could meet with the two together to ask the coaching questions above. Not only would you have invested in some of your existing leaders, but also now you would have some new leaders, in place and available for new ministries!

PAUL: Laity, Kim has suggested that your pastor choose five persons with whom to invest significant time, and then each of them choose one more. That is ten. Some of you may be ready to work alongside your pastor in mentoring other high-potential people. If ten of you worked alongside your pastor to mentor just one each, then this doubles the impact. And it aligns you and your pastor in a common focus on growing spiritual leaders.

KIM: One of the biggest challenges that most churches face is the culture of me-me-me. The pastor and the lay leaders have to model what it means to give this up and begin to live in such a way that our church culture can change: this is a place where you can be loved because that is what God calls us to be and do. As this attitude and the actions of love begin to spill from the leaders to others, it will eventually spill onto all of the people—maybe even those out in the community that you haven't met yet!!!

PAUL: As you describe this, a particular place comes to my mind.

KIM: Which church is that, Paul?

PAUL: Southwest Airlines. Seriously. Not a church, but it's an amazing organization, powerfully organized, with management focused on caring for employees, who care for other employees, who ultimately care for millions of customers. If you work for Southwest Airlines, you know without a doubt that your company loves you. They value you. They listen to your ideas and suggestions. They want you to be fulfilled in your work at Southwest. And why? Because they figured out that a happy work force is much more likely to be pleasant and responsive at a customer service counter or call center. A happy work force that is cared for instinctively knows that Southwest is about caring, and they pass it on to lots of strangers each year. Southwest is no "fly-by-night" airline; they are one of the big kids in the industry. But they are thriving in a dicey economy in which many others have faltered. This makes them a sort of "mainline denomination" that is bucking the negative trends in many of their peer organizations. And a big part of their success is that they love their leaders! (See Jody Hoffer Gittell, *The Southwest Airlines Way: Using the Power of Relationships to Achieve High Performance* [New York: McGraw Hill, 2003].)

KIM: I love flying Southwest! There is good positive energy among the flight crew, and I have never experienced an inhospitable flight. I'm sure that each crew member of Southwest is aware of the expectations for performance and how he or she fits into the overall picture of their industry. That is a realistic picture for how transformed congregations could behave!

PAUL: And they took a lot of it from Jesus' playbook.

KIM: Paul, I think we have painted a realistic picture of how a pastor and leader team can love a congregation. But I'm not naive enough to think that this can happen everywhere! Some churches out there are not ready to be loved.

PAUL: It's true. Sometimes this is due to trauma in the congregation. If one or more leaders have made inappropriate power moves in the recent past (ranging from autocratic style to sexual passes on parishioners by any leader—lay or clergy), the congregation may have difficulty relaxing so as to build a healthy partnership with future leaders. I would rather see such a congregation take the time and spend a little money to work with an interventionist-healer who can help them work through the trauma and heal as a church system. It is hard work, but it is immensely better than struggling for a generation or more with poorly tended wounds.

KIM: Sometimes one small group of folks are used to calling the shots, and they feel threatened by the thought that their church would grow to include other leaders and dilute their influence and dilute their internal sense of significance.

PAUL: And sometimes there are competing factions in a church. After a while, trust may disappear between the groups, so that they are barely civil on the surface, but functioning like the current U.S. Congress in every other respect.

KIM: When a pastor finds herself or himself in such situations, there are a few things to use to find a pathway to a new reality.

First, there is a spiritual dimension to every issue in a church's life—so prayer is a good first way to discover how best to love in such a context. Be open and vulnerable enough in your prayer life to look at yourself and wonder if you need work. Find a spiritual director or counselor to help you discover areas of concern that can help you open up to really loving others. Remember, what you want to experience is a relationship with God through Jesus that just spills over onto others. Try to identify where this is happening in your daily life.

PAUL: My "hard-to-love church" came early in my pastoral years. I was twenty-six and had never experienced such a community before. A spiritual director and a wise older pastor in the nearby county seat did wonders in helping me discern in prayer how best to love in that place. So I really endorse this idea.

KIM: A second thing to consider is that some leadership positions may need to be rotated within the congregation. It may be necessary to gently pull a few folks away from leadership—occasionally, though, you just have to lovingly *rip them away.*

PAUL: LOL.

KIM: Either way—the chaos that ensues will generally heal more quickly than you expect, and new leaders will rise to the surface! I have observed repeatedly that when one leader rotates, good leaders are waiting in the wings, ready for the change!

PAUL: Eventually, all leaders simply need to move on to another challenge. We once had a woman who ruled the church kitchen with an iron fist, which was not helping our church grow ministry. But we wanted to start a bookstore, and you need an iron fist to control inventory in a church bookstore. So, we gave the woman a new challenge, and it was a win-win for everybody. The ability to juggle leaders will vary by church and by denominational polity. But one way or another, in most church transformations, leaders will give up their posts as part of the transformation.

KIM: In other cases, a good pastor and a good congregation are just coming from really different places culturally or theologically. The match feels weird. Mismatches can hurt good pastors and cause them to find other avenues of work.

PAUL: Mismatches can also hurt good congregations and cause them to lose momentum. The best thing to do in such situations is for pastor and leaders to sit down and say, "Well, we are here together. It probably is not for the long term, but let's try to make the best of this time and find ways to make this work for the short run." During that time, it is often essential for the pastor to begin networking for another pastoral call or assignment. If the leaders know that this is going on, then very often they relax for a few months. If all parties can act like grown-ups, the church may be able to avoid a sudden pastoral change and spare everyone the trauma attached to that. If a church and pastor can grow in their capacity for loving through a difficult pastoral match, all parties will be stronger in the long run.

KIM: So, the surprise of God's activity is calling us to love one another, inviting us toward a difficult and revolutionary stance toward others.

PAUL: Which is the very last thing folks expect from us when they are behaving badly.

A conflict is often just the thing to crack the shells between us and to allow us to be real with one another and to offer the possibility for intimacy. A pastor that I coach described a very heated meeting with his church's leaders. Afterward, even though they all felt that they had been knocked down in the experience, they agreed to hang in there with one another and to honor one another with continued prayer and faithful communication. I believe that team is about to go to the next level in quality.

KIM: But it's their move, clearly, and in the wake of an argument, many folks do not make the right move. The strategic move is to practice spilling our love—caring, encouraging, accountable love—onto the people in our sphere of influence.

When this feels hard, then we should start with prayer, then move to open, honest conversations with those who will be able to listen. Through it all, keep God and God's desires for the congregation the focus of these conversations!

He was surrounded by the crowd when he was given the message, "Your mother and brothers and sisters are outside looking for you."

Jesus responded, "Who do you think are my mother and brothers?" Looking around, taking in everyone seated around him, he said, "Right here, right in front of you—my mother and my brothers." (Mark 3:31-35 *THE MESSAGE*)

He put a child in the middle of the room. Then, cradling the little one in his arms, he said, "Whoever embraces one of these children as I do embraces me, and far more than me—God who sent me." (Mark 9:36-37 *THE MESSAGE*)

Here is a simple rule of thumb for behavior: Ask yourself what you want people to do for you; then grab the initiative and do it for *them*! If you only love the lovable, do you expect a pat on the back? Run-of-the-mill sinners do that. If you only help those who help you, do you expect a medal? Garden-variety sinners do that. If you only give for what you hope to get out of it, do you think that's charity? The stingiest of pawnbrokers does that.

I tell you, love your enemies. Help and give without expecting a return. You'll never—I promise—regret it. Live out this God-created identity the way our Father lives toward us, generously and graciously, even when we're at our worst. Our Father is kind; you be kind.

Don't pick on people, jump on their failures, criticize their faults—unless, of course, you want the same treatment. Don't condemn those who are down; that hardness can boomerang. Be easy on people; you'll find life a lot easier. (Luke 6:31-37 *THE MESSAGE*)

For the message you gave me, I gave them; / And they took it, and were convinced / That I came from you. / They believed that you sent me. / I pray for them. / ... Holy Father, guard them as they pursue this life / That you conferred as a gift through me, / So they can be one heart and mind. (John 17:8-11 *THE MESSAGE*)

So he got up from the supper table, set aside his robe, and put on an apron. Then he poured water into a basin and began to wash the feet of the disciples, drying them with his apron. (John 13:3-5 *THE MESSAGE*)

Three

LOVE YOUR COMMUNITY

Jeanne is pastor to a ninety-five-member congregation in a small-town setting. She is a second-career pastor, and this is her first church. When she came to this town, she immediately saw great possibilities for community ministry, and she fell in love with the place!

Soon after arriving, Jeanne joined several groups: the Community Association, the Genealogical Society, and the Homemakers. By means of these organizations, she was able to build relationships and get to know some of the issues and concerns in the community.

She also began to connect with folks in the community who were not associated with any church, especially when they were in the hospital or when she discovered a crisis. This networking helped her spread the word that the church she serves is for everyone! She made herself available for weddings and funerals for anyone in need.

Jeanne's church had a daycare ministry, overflowing with children five days a week. Not one family from the daycare was active in her church. She took the opportunity to get to know the parents of the daycare children, especially since most of them were not active in any church.

Quite a few townspeople have now claimed Jeanne as their pastor. The added benefit for the congregation is that now they can see what they didn't see earlier: the possibilities and potential for ministry in this community. And when their friends brag about how Jeanne came to see them, the church members feel proud to be associated with their church.

KIM: I have been living through an interesting crossroad in my life. Recently, after years of coming to every town with a ready-made church, Gary and I worked on national projects for the denomination, which moved us to Nashville for a few years. The differences were numerous: we lived in an urban setting for the first time, for the first few months in an apartment setting, and we left our sons in another state! We had to go looking for a church, along with all the other things one looks for in a new city. It's all been very strange. For weeks, I wondered, "What do I need to do to fall in love with my new community?"

PAUL: Eat the food, in all of its variety and wonder! Your West End neighborhood in Nashville had some really interesting places to eat!

I made the move also to central-city life about six years ago, and it's been a lot of fun. In my first year in Washington DC, a woman from the Gallup Organization worked with me in hosting a couple of community conversations with groups of relative strangers in my neighborhood, asking a similar question to yours—how do you make a new city your home? Their answers were eye opening.

KIM: Well, in my case, first I needed to get familiar with my surroundings and look for those things that life seems to demand—grocery store, doctor, dentist, gas station, shopping in general. Finding a good salon for a haircut was very encouraging!

PAUL: I will travel halfway across the universe for a decent haircut. In my current situation, all the way into Virginia!

KIM: It is amazing how the haircut is a symbol of home! I also spent time trying to notice the people around me, especially in the weeks before I began working full time. We lived in a complex that houses university students and folks who work at the hospital on the next block. I had some quick conversations in the elevator, but building relationships in that community was not easy.

PAUL: It is not easy. It can be eerily quiet in an elevator full of people in my building. I sometimes wonder what would happen if Tony Campolo moved in and started singing "You Are My Sunshine" on our elevator each morning.

Building socials and the condo resident association meetings are like gold for relationship building. And the grills! When I was at your place a couple of summers ago, down on the community patio by the grills, I visited with one of your neighbors and discovered he lives part time in Nashville and part time a few blocks from me in Washington.

KIM: I agree, the grills were a wonderful meeting place! But it was always difficult to get people to look at me when I walked in the halls. We eventually made a few acquaintances and had folks over for dinner. We also provided guest rooms for out-of-town coworkers who would come in for meetings occasionally, which provides some sense of community for all of us!

It also seems important for me to get a sense of the needs of a community, in order for me to find my place. Early on, I discovered that Nashville has a significant homeless population, and many of these folks are on the street corners with a small newspaper that they sell for one dollar.

PAUL: We have a paper like that in DC, too. It's a great little business.

KIM: Each newspaper they sell earns them matching funds, so they can begin to rebuild their lives. So, we're buying newspapers. We watched local news channels and learned about the way the community functions. It all takes a little time and effort.

We also visited churches, trying to find one that fit us. We both have an overwhelming need to worship God on a regular basis in an energized way—traditional or contemporary doesn't really matter. What matters is whether we connect with God in meaningful ways. We looked for a congregation that wanted to make a difference in its community. So a hospitable, welcoming congregation was our first clue about how they view themselves and the world around them.

PAUL: I know you found a good one. You talked about it all the time.

KIM: We loved our Nashville church. And recently we have helped bring a free store to life in our church's community. We volunteered regularly and discovered even more ways to be a blessing in a new neighborhood.

PAUL: Looking for a church was one of the most notable missing items from the nesting agenda when we interviewed folks in Washington DC. We discovered that most people assumed there is not much real community to be found at church. Many folks assumed that bars and nightclubs are better places for building community. Bars *and* churches can each offer pretty superficial encounters. But occasionally you find more.

KIM: Paul, that's a really sad statement about the church today. I'm finding it is actually a practice in boldness to move into a new community.

PAUL: And apparently, it is a practice in extraordinary boldness for many people to get up the nerve to walk cold into a strange church!

KIM: Yes! I found that out while I was looking for new friends and new places to belong. I came up against situations where it is necessary for others to make room for me! I can see why a lot of folks just stick to themselves and don't interact with existing groups and fellowships. It is very hard to be the new person looking for a new place to be when everyone around you is happy about where they are!

So, how can congregations and pastors learn to love the people in their communities?

PAUL: It won't happen by studying a fancy demographic report in the church boardroom. I can tell you that much. And this from a guy who could happily waste an afternoon on a demographics website!

KIM: There is a place for sitting in the boardroom to learn from demographic research and identifying needs and determining a process to implement goals. But too often we never move beyond discovery to embrace action.

PAUL: And if we do not have meaningful relationships with real people, sprinkled around the community—where we know their kids' names, their current life challenges, and their favorite movie—we will likely not get far in terms of understanding our community. It is hard to complete any meaningful discovery phase about a place until we really have made some friends there. Loving statistics and loving people—these are different sports.

KIM: In Jeanne's experience, it was her coming to town that opened up the eyes of the congregation to what was so familiar around them. As she shared her experiences out in the community, surprisingly the members of her church began to see their town with new eyes.

It may sound cliché, but would anyone in your community truly miss your congregation if it were gone? Have you loved your community in such a way that you have made a difference? I recently learned of a congregation that has a letter from the local government thanking them for making reduced crime among teens a reality because of their youth center. That's loving your community!

PAUL: The thing that strikes me about Jeanne is that she led. Leaders lead. And it is not good for leaders to try to lead where they themselves have not gone. By deciding that she would love her new community, she opened the doors of possibility for her church to fall in love again with the community beyond its walls.

Are there any scriptures that drive your thinking about this?

KIM: I think about Psalm 133:1: "How very good and pleasant it is / when kindred live together in unity!" (NRSV). Matthew 18:20 reminds us: "For where two or three are gathered in my name, I am there among them" (NRSV). I notice when I read these verses, and many others like them, that the Scriptures never define exactly who is a part of any community.

PAUL: Interesting. When I read those verses, I have been programmed to think about a faith community already gathered and organized, but that may be a bit of *eisogesis* on my part: reading my assumptions into the Scriptures. Those verses could just as easily apply to positive connection with our neighbors beyond the church rolls.

KIM: The New Testament never gives the sense that only one religious affiliation should come together or that one defined ethnic group should come together, or one age group, or one group of a similar social standing or sexual orientation. The descriptive words are very vague about this. I like how Tom Hawkins puts it:

> Scripture tells the story of God's persistent effort to invite all creatures into communion. God ceaselessly creates community where there is alienation, reconciliation where there is enmity, redemption where there is bondage. This love of God overcomes the fears that prevent us from experiencing community. "Beloved, let us love one another, because love is from God.... God is love, and those who abide in love abide in God, and God abides in them.... There is no fear in love, but perfect love casts out fear" (1 John 4:7, 16b, 18). (Thomas R. Hawkins, *Cultivating Christian Community* [Nashville: Discipleship Resources, 2001], 9)

35

I see two ways that churches think about *community*. First of all, we use the word to refer to a particular faith community—the members and attendees of any given congregation. But when we think of *community* primarily in this way, then we easily become inward-focused and concentrate our ministry and community energy on those who are already in.

PAUL: This sort of parish is completely defined by the list in the back of the church pictorial directory. It is clearly inadequate. It falls far short of what God is calling us to be/do.

This is especially tough for congregations that began as ethnic enclaves, such as German Lutherans, often formed with a mission to preserve an internal community identity more than to evangelize outsiders. Now, many decades later, nearly all of their descendants have merged into the larger culture, and they may be left without a purpose to exist—and with no evangelistic DNA upon which to draw!

KIM: I coached a pastor who was serving a church with a very inward understanding of community. Church members wanted their pastor to bring in children and youth from the neighborhood so that they could have a sense of a future for their congregation. But the demographic research for this congregation showed that the largest group of available children and youth in that community were the sons and daughters of the Hispanic folks who worked in the area. So, the pastor was ready to develop after-school programs to these families, but guess what? The congregation said, "We don't want *those* people here!"

PAUL: I used not to believe stories like that. But you get around enough, and you see it all. I know a church in Alabama that stopped having vacation Bible school for fear that a black child would attend. Better to do no ministry at all than to risk certain people showing up. There were a few folks in a liberal church I worked with who worried that a more contemporary style of worship service might actually attract Republicans. In both cases, people were looking for designer churches, where the homogeneity of the faith community's demographic mix was more important than the church's mission to the world beyond its walls. There are reasonable psychological explanations for such behavior. But it is still inexcusable.

KIM: I have to wonder what people think heaven will look like. Who do they expect to find there? Wouldn't it be great to experience some of heaven on earth?

The second way we think about community is in reference to the neighborhood around the church building or some other significant neighborhood in the immediate community.

PAUL: And I would add a third way; sometimes *community* refers to a virtual neighborhood. I live in DC's Chinatown. The Chinese Community Church meets one block away. Since most Chinese people no longer live in Chinatown, most participants drive in from all over a large region. The church has a virtual neighborhood that comprises Chinese Americans, Chinese citizens (working for a time in DC), and those who love them within a metropolitan region of five million people. A virtual neighborhood can be just as tangible as a geographic neighborhood. Focusing on a tangible people group can help a church define its parish area and focus its outreach beyond the church's walls.

KIM: That's true, but I still think we have to take seriously the neighbors God has placed on our doorstep. There may be some wonderful surprises there! It is too easy to go fishing all over the two-county area and to walk or drive past a lot of neighbors. Jesus in Acts 1:8 tells us: "You will receive power when the Holy Spirit has come upon you; and you will be my witnesses in Jerusalem, in all Judea and Samaria, and to the ends of the earth" (NRSV). He did not give them the option of skipping over Jerusalem or Samaria in their ministry quest. Why would Jesus have gone to all the trouble to mingle with Samaritans and to tell a parable with a *good* Samaritan as the protagonist? I think he was saying that we should not create designer parishes. We are called to the people around us as we find them.

PAUL: I am thinking about Texas congressional districts. I suppose we can gerrymander our parish areas just as they do political districts in order to find a people mix that suits our purposes.

KIM: That is just wrong. We should think of our community first as Jerusalem—the people who live around us! God calls us to pay close attention to the folks who live where we live. And that proximity provides good opportunity for finding things in common. This is where any local congregation can make the most difference! I get the virtual parish thing, but I just don't want to see us using that as an excuse for ignoring the next-door neighbors.

PAUL: I am amazed at how many communities are filling up with new people groups—people who used to live *over there* now belong *over here*. All the sheep are out of their fences, grazing and settling wherever they please. This is pointing toward that magical moment, which comes on or around my eightieth birthday, when there will no longer be any ethnic majority in the United States. I hope I live to see this. Many of our local communities passed that landmark moment years ago. Even Washington DC—which was 70 percent African American thirty years ago—now has no ethnic majority.

A block down from the Chinese church is the congregation that invites me to more events than any other congregation in DC. I wrote about them in my last book. This congregation also has strong ethnic roots and comes from a tradition with a very weak history of evangelism. I refer to the historic Sixth and I Synagogue, a congregation that has truly adopted our neighborhood, all of us: Jewish and not. They have created the closest thing to a truly inclusive community center in Chinatown. I have attended many interesting events and activities there, some distinctively Jewish and others not. Concerts, authors, cooking classes—Sixth and I is a hopping place most evenings. Obviously, I am not Jewish; nevertheless they have helped me (and a lot of others in my neighborhood) feel a part of that place. It then should surprise no one that this downtown congregation packs their sanctuary for the Jewish high holy days, even having to use a ticket system to manage the crowds.

KIM: Earlier, I mentioned the three-point circuit of congregations that my husband, Gary, served in rural Pennsylvania. When we arrived, there were about forty older folks in the pews at the largest of the three churches. Within a year, there were about 120 folks of all ages in those pews. By the start of the third year, the church had partnered with the local high school to start a S.A.D.D. chapter for the neighborhood (Students Against Drunk Driving). They hired a youth worker and renovated an empty storefront to run a youth club. By the sixth year, they had taken over another storefront to offer the neighborhood a thrift shop. The most basic change that happened was a shift from looking inward ("How can we care about us?") to outward ("How can we impact this community for God?")! The congregation learned to extend their sense of community to include everyone!

PAUL: Was there any particular strategy that helped turn their eyes from themselves to their neighbors?

KIM: It really started with "funeral evangelism"—being available to conduct funerals for the families who had no connection to the church. The local funeral director provided ample opportunities to reach people. Gary's availability transferred to the women's group, who was willing to host some funeral dinners—a great time for building relationships with folks. Before we knew it, the church was growing, and the congregation was making room for new folks.

PAUL: Kim, as you know, I recently published another book: *We Refused to Lead a Dying Church!* It is a collection of real stories from all sorts of community contexts about how churches were reborn against all odds. In every case, part of the story was that they reconnected with their communities.

KIM: I loved reading the stories in this book, Paul. Over and over again I was encouraged that God has work for us to do in our communities. About a year ago, I received a speeding ticket—and I was guilty. So I took the ticket, paid my fine, and signed up for online traffic school, which is supposed to help keep your insurance rates from rising. Within the previous five years I had taught two teenage sons to drive, so I figured I wouldn't really learn much, but I did learn one very significant thing. If one practices keeping enough space in front of one's own vehicle, the chances of an accident or any driving mishap are significantly reduced. Now, I will admit, practicing this is a lot different from learning it. It is nearly impossible to keep the proper amount of space in front of you, especially if you drive in a city, because everyone else is looking to hog your space. So I find myself constantly trying to make enough room around my vehicle. This whole idea of making room has really impacted the way I think about living my faith as well.

When congregations apply the idea of making room, the space we create is ultimately used by someone else, not ourselves. In driving, the principle is primarily to keep me safe, but it helps keep the people around me safe, too. Apply this to our faith journey: as we become more aware of the folks around us, we begin to notice what they need. Awareness of those around us is no longer just the job of the ushers, greeters, and pastor. Since my driver's class, I'm more conscious of the need to make room for those around me, especially in worship. I am becoming more open and aware of the people around me— even when I'm the visitor!

PAUL: At my church, we take five minutes before every service to find someone located in the nearby space that we do not know well and have a meaningful conversation. Personally, I find it very helpful.

KIM: There are lots of ways for congregations to fall in love with their communities, but first we have to *notice* that the neighborhood is there!

PAUL: Sometimes, a simple prayer walk with a group of church leaders around a few blocks near the church building is a great way to begin noticing. Cheri Holdridge, a pastor in Toledo, has written a helpful little guide, *How to Organize a Prayer Walk*. It is available, alongside the study guide for this book, as a free download at www.epicentergroup.org.

Then, beyond noticing people, we have to find ways to talk to one another. Often we need to work on something together in order to form relationships across the various kinds of boundaries that exist between the congregation and the community. The boundaries can be socioeconomic, political, ethnic, and generational—you name it.

One of the churches I work with has a tagline: "We love Cubs fans. We love Sox fans." Imagine a church of Cubs fans that finds itself in a neighborhood of Sox fans. (NOTE: This is a multisite church that planted its first three worship venues on the north side of the city, in Cubs territory. However, in 2012, they moved squarely into Sox territory with their fourth site.)

KIM: I can imagine talk of relocation.

PAUL: And I can imagine the pastor getting in hot water for fraternizing with all those Sox fans. But if he doesn't mix with Sox fans, how on earth can he lead a Cubs church with any integrity to love its neighbors? Finally, for me, it boils down to this: *the leader has to go there if she expects to lead a church to go there.* That's the deal. And she or he can always take a friend! In fact, that is even better.

I have spent considerable ink over the years throwing out ideas for how church leaders can network in communities, courting a community if you will, in order to fall in love. Since so much of my work lately has been with church-planting pastors, developing relationships in the community is a very obvious and basic task. But every pastor is needed here, and the lay leadership is needed here! In all of this, we have to relax and be ourselves: take notice of our neighbors, and then find ways to talk with them, to listen to them, to discover and to think with them about issues of common interest.

Kim, you have been a part of two church plants—so you know something about working a neighborhood. Are there any basic points you would offer to leaders, lay or clergy, who feel a little put off by this challenge, for the person who may be somewhat introverted, or for the person who may not be experienced in community networking?

KIM: Well, the most obvious thing would be just to get out there! And travel in pairs, especially if this feels a little scary. Decide which people you will visit first—possibly social service people, such as educators, law enforcement, and medical folks, who know the community. Ask God to prepare your path. Tell people you are from XYZ Church and that your church is engaged in a process of listening and discernment about how you can help make the community stronger. And listen to what people have to say. They will be impressed that you came by in most cases.

Overall, I think people are looking for Christians to be genuine people who want to interact with others in real ways—not fake smiling people . . .

PAUL: . . . or, God help us, know-it-all people who offer only critique or prefabricated answers to questions we haven't even heard yet.

KIM: Yes, we have to be real! Find a coffee shop where you can take your laptop or some correspondence and just stay there for an hour or so to work. Go there several times a week. Get to know the baristas by name and use their names when you chat with them. It is amazing the kind of network you can develop over time because the staff will begin to connect you to other customers, too.

PAUL: I coach one pastor whose "office" consists of multiple neighborhood coffee shops. He has a Tuesday afternoon spot, a Wednesday morning spot, and so forth. It saves him office rent, and it keeps him immersed in community.

KIM: It is possible for inward-focused people to learn to be more outward-focused just by remembering that you are God's hands and feet in your neighborhood. When you eat in a restaurant, ask your server if he or she has any prayer concerns you can offer when you say grace. When you return to eat again, ask about that concern. Make eye contact with the folks in the grocery store, share a friendly greeting, try to smile more, and look for ways to help others with simple things! So often we are walking around so deep inside our own heads that we forget that everyone we meet also has a story to tell and that each person may need to hear of God's grace and love toward him or her.

PAUL: It's not really my style to ask for prayer requests from a server in a restaurant. Different personalities I guess. But playful and gracious inter-action with a server may cause one to stand out favorably from among the other customers—and especially if the place is not too busy, the server will sometimes begin to share about herself or himself. One server in an Alabama diner last year shared so much about her difficult life situation that the pastor I was with did actually end up asking how we could pray for her.

In terms of more organized interface with community, consider these possibilities:

- Deliver free sack lunches door to door in a public housing proj-ect as a gift from your church! And then, before you leave each front porch, ask if there is anything you could pray for regarding the family's needs. It will vary by context, but in some neigh-borhoods, 90 percent of the people will accept the lunches and two-thirds will take you up on the prayer offer. The key is to focus on the person encountered more than on the church you are a part of. It is about them.

- Have a group from your church take a box of Frisbees to a park or a beach and start playing with them. Kids will join you. And some adults. Frisbees are cheap and are a lot of fun. Put the church's name on them, and then give them away at the end of the time.

- Offer community-based short-term activities that meet your community at the point of their most pressing personal inter-ests. I am working this year with a church seeking to reach into a new zip code with a high population of non-Christian immi-grants and very rich people. Most folks in this community are not shopping for a church. So the church trained a team to hold community conversations, both individually and in groups, with a couple hundred folks in order to discover opportunities for the church to connect with their lives. Preliminary minis-try emphases that look promising are: (1) children's recreation and spirituality development, (2) stress reduction/meditation/ yoga and possibly mixing yoga with forms of Christian liturgy, (3) serving others, (4) rites of passage for life transitions, and (5) reconnecting with nature. The faith community that emerges from all this, they will call *Imagine.* Imagine will sponsor some ongoing groups and special events related to these themes. But please notice that they are not adding a typical worship service in this zip code yet. Almost no one is looking for Christian worship in the neighborhood, so they are seeking to build relationships at this point. (When they are ready to begin worship, they may know several hundred people.)

KIM: I would think that this would be a good practice before any established church starts any new groups or worship services, so that they can make sure they are meeting real needs within the community. There's nothing worse than offering something that no one wants or needs!

PAUL: And many churches have become specialists in offering that which no one in the community wants or needs.

KIM: You know, Paul, we never really know how God uses the smiles and kind words and offers of concern toward other people, and I would much rather trust in God's growth of the seeds I throw out than keep those seeds for myself!

I want to underline that it is important for the pastor to hold the leaders accountable to this kind of behavior. Too many churches talk big but never get around to taking action. At your meetings, begin your time together with an opportunity to share stories of how relationships are being built with folks in your community. Share places where there seems to be openness to working together. Also share the places where there is resistance. As you learn what people are doing in their daily lives to impact your community for Christ, you may find ways to be more intentional!

God surprises us by placing us in communities that need to hear good news! We respond strategically by noticing the community, learning its needs, and finding some ways to respond that are helpful and genuine. We experience great surprise when we begin to understand what God is doing!

PAUL: And of course, nothing was more basic to Jesus' playbook as a movement leader than to hang out with community people. It got him in hot water with the institutional religious folks, but it also was a key component that empowered his movement.

Jesus and his disciples were at home having supper with a collection of disreputable guests. Unlikely as it seems, more than a few of them had become followers. The religion scholars and Pharisees saw him keeping this kind of company and lit into his disciples: "What kind of example is this, acting cozy with the riffraff?" Jesus, overhearing, shot back, "Who needs a doctor: the healthy or the sick? I'm here inviting the sin-sick, not the spiritually-fit." (Mark 2:15-17 *THE MESSAGE*)

That evening, after the sun was down, they brought sick and evil-afflicted people to him, the whole city lined up at his door! (Mark 1:32 *THE MESSAGE*)

Someone saw them…and the word got around. From the surrounding towns people went out on foot, running, and got there ahead of them. When Jesus arrived, he saw this huge crowd. At the sight of them, his heart broke—like sheep with no shepherd they were. He went right to work teaching them. (Mark 6:33-34 *THE MESSAGE*)

When Jesus got to the tree, he looked up and said, "Zacchaeus, hurry down. Today is my day to be a guest in your home." Zacchaeus scrambled out of the tree, hardly believing his good luck, delighted to take Jesus home with him. Everyone who saw the incident was indignant and grumped, "What business does he have getting cozy with this crook?"

Zacchaeus just stood there, a little stunned. He stammered apologetically, "Master, I give away half my income to the poor—and if I'm caught cheating, I pay four times the damages."

Jesus said, "Today is salvation day in this home!" (Luke 19:5-9 *THE MESSAGE*)

Four

TREAT URGENCY AS A GIFT!

Phyllis has never felt fully embraced by Colonial Hills Church. She is the first fe-male senior pastor, and no one is complaining. Yet she senses some sort of hesitancy, as if she is constantly running for office. She has the office; she was installed as pastor here eight months ago. Yet she still feels as if she is in the midst of a constant political campaign. She has pondered this at length, deciding that perhaps she is still campaigning for people's hearts. Her name is listed in the worship order and posted on the church sign, but she senses that many people are still ponder-ing whether or not fully to own her as their pastor. The fact that her much-loved pastoral predecessor remains a prominent resident in the community further com-plicates the process of the church embracing her leadership.

When Phyllis answered God's call to pastoral ministry, she had no clue that she was going into politics, in that she must effectively campaign and rally a co-alition of leaders around issues that both she and they consider urgent. She has always considered politics a bit distasteful. But, like a woman running for county commissioner, in the last few weeks, Phyllis has held a dozen special gatherings in the homes of various church members. In each of these meetings, she listened carefully to people's concerns and then watched how people responded to her varied responses. One of the most common topics mentioned in these meetings was the dwindling number of children and youth at Colonial Hills. Where once youth and children's programs were signature ministries for the church, now most activities and classes attract fewer kids than the critical mass necessary to energize children and their families.

Phyllis began to see ministry to children and youth as an anxiety magnet and an opportunity. Not many folks were volunteering to help or to lead at this point, but she realized that almost any new thing that she proposed would stand a better chance if she framed it as addressing a situation that bothered many folks. The anxiety could then be harnessed as urgency to fuel the new proposals, changes, or initiatives.

PAUL: I like the way Phyllis thinks.

It reminds me of William Bridges's classic advice to those who lead through organizational transitions: "Sell the problem" (*Managing Transitions* [Philadelphia: Da Capo Press, 2009], 26)! Often our first instinct is to say, "Now, now. It's okay that you have no viable children's ministry. You have other great gifts as a congregation." We say such things to relieve anxiety and to boost the congregation's self-esteem. But in Phyllis's case, to relieve this anxiety would be to undermine the greatest single leverage point for change that she has been handed at Colonial Hills Church!

KIM: In the book *Switch: How to Change Things When Change Is Hard,* Chip Heath and Dan Heath talk about "rallying the herd" (New York: Broadway Books, 2010, chap. 10). The key thing to discern when rallying a herd is *what one thing will get people motivated to change by pointing them in one direction.*

PAUL: That's a fun book, Kim. Harnessing and riding Colonial Hills's church anxiety about a dwindling children's population is one way that we can "motivate the elephant" (p. 84), to use another metaphor from *Switch*. In the case of the people at Colonial Hills, the widely shared anxiety about the church and children probably masks some more fundamental anxieties—about their own aging and mortality, strained relationships with their own children, or their loss of personal power reflected in the marginalization of their faith community in the larger social sphere. People's "presenting issues" may be rooted in all sorts of life experiences and emotions. Nonetheless, if children's ministry turns around on Phyllis's watch, her leadership credibility will be established, and she will be in a stronger position to lead change on other fronts. The majority of folks will never volunteer to help with children's ministry. But this also doesn't matter: Phyllis needs just a dozen or so volunteers to get started.

What does matter is this: Phyllis has discovered a way to rally folks at Colonial Hills, a way that harnesses their worst fears and drives them in a positive direction.

KIM: One pastor I worked with used the phrase "It's later than we think" as a rallying cry. The congregation paid attention to what he had to say next!

PAUL: In order for Phyllis to lead Colonial Hills effectively in a rapidly changing community and century, there will have to be various and continuous changes and innovations. By choosing to lift up the *stated concern* about the church's need for a more effective ministry to children and youth, Phyllis accomplishes three things:

1. She reminds them that business as usual is not a viable option.

2. She claims an issue that could be the nine-volt battery to drive consensus around any number of initiatives that she and key leaders wish to pursue—so long as they are clearly connected to addressing this problem in the church's life.

3. When clear improvements and accomplishments occur, she is in business to lead on other fronts, with increased leadership credibility.

KIM: A fourth thing that Phyllis accomplishes is having a line now marked in the sand by which evaluation can happen. When clear direction does not exist, there is no way to know if we're getting anywhere!

PAUL: Yes. Progress documented not only encourages the body but also gives momentum for the next steps required.

Whether we like it or not, political reality always informs the route by which any group of people can move toward any particular action. Any leader who ignores, denies, or resists this reality, does so at his or her peril.

I live in DC, the capital of the perpetual political campaign. Church politics usually does not get as brutal as the national political game. However, I have learned never to underestimate the capacity of church people to play rough politically.

According to a common cliché, Washington is broken. In reality, most people don't really know my hometown, except the way it gets spun on cable news. Washington is simply a big sports arena for a national game. The arena is not perfect, but whatever discord or gridlock we have in Washington politics is mostly a matter of the anxieties and agendas folks bring to town from Idaho, Texas, and New York. (And of course, a few very rich people and organizations fuel much of the discord, throwing their money to political machines and media mouthpieces that will help make them richer and more powerful over time.)

Similarly, we often hear that organized religion is broken. But again, most church dysfunctions are endemic not to faith itself but to the junk we bring to church with us. Either clergy or laity can fall into an unhealthy relationship with the church, in which the church becomes a stage for personal power, agenda, and significance rather than being focused on God's will.

KIM: "What's in it for me?" is the cry that hurts our country as well as our congregations. In almost every place, there are a few people who have wrapped up their egos and agendas with that of their churches.

PAUL: It is easy to hijack a church with pet agendas. Some folks feel like little fish in the sea and find the church to be a place where they can think of themselves as big fish. In the case of paid staff, the church is their economic livelihood. I have known many long-term staff who serve humbly and sacrificially for decades. I have known other staff members who work for years to cultivate the church, almost like a bonsai tree, to conform to their personal tastes and abilities to manage.

KIM: What is notable about bonsai trees is that they are cultivated to be smaller than they otherwise would be.

PAUL: Interesting.

Now, *all of us* come to church (or mosque or synagogue) with our fears, our needs, our prejudices, and a variety of agendas. None of us comes to church empty-handed in this regard. And yet most folks, even with the mix of motivations going on within, do not seek inappropriate control of the church. The majority of people at most churches just want to get along, to worship God, to see the church make a meaningful difference in the lives of people. Often, however, these good folks also want to avoid the messy work of confronting the few folks with inappropriate boundaries and control issues.

KIM: It always amazes me, when I talk with the "most folks" you mentioned, how often they are blissfully unaware of the political nature of their congregations. They may not even realize that the badly behaving folks are controlling the day.

PAUL: I saw that in one of the churches featured in my book *We Refused to Lead a Dying Church!* The old guard was not well networked with the new people, and this helped quarantine a very volatile church conflict from infecting newer members. Just the opposite of Fox News churning up mischief every night, church politics can go underground and quiet for years, so that newcomers are clueless.

KIM: "Most folks" just want a place to be comfortable and to stay connected to God as they make their way through life.

PAUL: So, in terms of the political landscape of a typical religious congregation, let's think in terms of three basic players:

- Most folks, the crowd. (This includes most newcomers in the last few years.)
- The people with need for power in the church, who may (or may not) be disturbed by and acting in response to some offense, real or perceived.
- The pastor (who sometimes also has weird power needs).

KIM: I can't help mentioning that hiring a coach may be the right way for a pastor to explore his or her own weird power needs!

PAUL: Definitely.

In the early days of a church transformation, the pastoral leader and the emerging team of bright-eyed people almost invariably have to dance with several of the power people. Over time, some of these relationships may become strained. However, if the pastor builds a strong relationship with the larger crowd (and with new folks coming into the system), she or he can usually weather a cantankerous power broker or two, *for a season*. Eventually, there will have to be enough new direction, new faces, and new money that the church is able to risk rupturing its relationship with an unhappy power person. The power person knows this at some level and may become increasingly agitated as the church system grows to include new people with more loyalty to the pastor than to the carefully cultivated status quo. Power people may see it to their advantage to do whatever they can do to resist growth and to discourage new people. From a church transformation perspective, it may be to the advantage of the pastor to continue to humor and tolerate the overbearing power person until the pastor has enough momentum to win a showdown. She or he may also work to gather and develop the new guard at some distance from the power people for a season.

KIM: In one of the churches we served, one gentleman fit your description of a power person. Gary had to do the face-to-face confrontation when the guy instigated a petition-signing meeting at the local restaurant. Luckily there was enough positive momentum for Gary to disband the opposition party and avoid any long-term problems.

PAUL: Sometimes the showdown never comes. The power people just read their diminished odds and choose to fold, or to lie low until the next pastor comes along. At this point, they may make peace with the church's leadership and make themselves helpful again. Or they may quit the church. Or they may simply lie in wait until some new controversy comes along, giving them a new pot to stir.

KIM: The latter possibility could get tricky. I don't know any of those who "lie in wait" that can do so quietly. I can also say that nearly every church transformation story has the reality of people leaving the church. As painful as this is, it usually ends up being a good thing.

PAUL: In addition to these basic players, there are likely pockets of passion and special interests within the congregation. These special-interest communities may include (but are not limited to):

- Those who have spent considerable time in personal spiritual development: the Pietists.
- Those who are passionate about music, often about a particular type or tradition of music: the Artistic Performers and Patrons.
- Those who are at church because of their kids: the Youth Groupies.
- Those who have spent time in community and world-service activities, in ministries of both mercy and justice: the Mission Advocates.

- Those who are drawn to church most powerfully because of the social connections and community discovered there: the Partiers.

- Those who have rallied around a hot-button theological or political issue, often originating beyond the congregation: the Crusaders.

- Those who crave special attention from the pastor as powerfully as some folks crave crack cocaine: the Puppies. (Craving attention is an addiction, as surely as craving power, and not one you may wish to try to cure in your first six months as pastor in a new place.)

KIM: It is fun to put faces with all these categories that you mentioned!

PAUL: You have met them all?

KIM: All of them.

PAUL: I've got some faces in my mind right now, too. I encourage leaders to think about the people inside their church and to think about which alliances they belong to. You can work with any and all of the above special-interest groups to grow and develop a church. Each group feels anxiety or urgency around certain issues. I urge any leaders (lay or pastor) seeking to move a church toward new life to pay close attention to these issues! They are a gift. These issues are like the controls of an airplane. When people tell you what worries and motivates them, they are handing you the control wheel!

When I was a small child, around six, our family had a friend with a Cessna, and sometimes he would hand me the control wheel. When someone hands you the control wheel, please pay attention. They are giving you a chance to fly the plane!

KIM: That's scary—a six-year-old flying an airplane.

PAUL: It's scary at any age to discover that you are flying the plane. Some folks never get comfortable with it, and so they never take the control wheel. They never accept the call to lead. And their churches fly chaotically.

KIM: Or crash? Paul, you were talking about special-interest groups. Some folks belong to more than one interest group.

PAUL: That can be a very good thing.

KIM: Crashing?

PAUL: No, varied connections! The more varied connections we have in a church's life, the easier it may be for us to adjust and hang on when one of those connections is stressed. Church transformation is guaranteed to stress some connections!

Most folks are lovable, interesting, and gifted in varied ways. A few are not so lovable! They are probably highly committed to a particular aspect of church life. You get between people and what they want most from their church, and they may become meaner than the devil.

KIM: And often very vocal about their own needs! When a church turns around from slow decline to growth, some special-interest folks may feel that the church they have loved is threatened, even under siege. Some of them will fight the changes.

PAUL: A few of them will fight the pastor.

However, most folks will weather a church transition and hang in there with the pastor *if* they perceive that there is more to gain by holding on and adjusting to a new day than by leaving or simply being cranky. A church's leadership team in a season of transformation should see to it that most folks clearly have more to gain than to lose—and help them discover this for themselves. It is important to let leaders know that their positive words about change will do amazing things for the rest of the congregation! One leader's negative words can kill the whole thing.

KIM: I find that the relational equity that a pastor has with people is helpful at this point. If the folks trust the pastor, if the folks know that the pastor has their needs at heart, and if the pastor has spiritual credibility with a good group of people, then the disruption is much less. In some situations, it may be helpful to ensure good relational equity before trying to change. This relational equity is also true for the lay leaders of the congregation. I will echo the necessity for the clergy and lay leaders to speak positively about what is going on. Everyone else will take their cues from the leaders' behavior!

PAUL: Yes, no one wants to mess up an otherwise great relationship with a pastor or leaders. So those relationships could help some folks process difficult changes. Yet we do need to remember that in most church transformation journeys, a few of our special-interest friends will leave in frustration, sometimes making a very noisy and dramatic exit.

KIM: There is always that!

PAUL: When we pastors are running for office—during the first months *in the office*—one of our main challenges is to cobble together a coalition of friends from the above groups with whom we can constructively collaborate and who will bless new directions and innovations in the church's life. This requires considerable listening and relationship building, so that we can discern the possibilities for rallying a coalition. In Phyllis's case, she discovered a pretty wide variety of folks whose fears, needs, prejudices, and agendas converged on the loss of the children. So rebuilding children's ministry became a macro issue for Colonial Hills Church, an issue that wove diverse constituencies together.

The presenting issues of anxiety will vary from church to church. They are often related to some aspect of the church's life that folks perceive as diminished from earlier times. They may also be related to a highly visible institutional crisis, such as a decaying facility or a budget deficit.

KIM: They also may be related to a community crisis, such as a significant ethnic shift within the community, a new industry and influx of outsiders, or grief that so many local young people leave their hometowns to work elsewhere.

PAUL: One of my friends became pastor of an old prestigious (and declining) church where the staff payroll was greater than the church's income from all sources. In order to maintain all the staff, the church was bleeding down its savings and had only a few years left before the crash. My friend seized upon the anxiety around the impending fiscal Armageddon. She saw this crisis as a gift. She harnessed the anxiety into urgency about making long-needed staff changes, bringing the budget nearer to balance, and also giving the church a more effective staff. In so doing, she laid the foundation for an amazing turnaround. A major hurricane then hit the city, creating the necessary chaos for the turnaround to be completed.

KIM: In the Great Recession, we heard a lot of these stories, of chaos and crisis offering great opportunities. In some ways, challenging financial issues help churches focus on community-minded ministries rather than inward programs!

PAUL: There is almost always a silver lining in a crisis. Crisis is opportunity. It is our friend. When we as leaders are prayerfully attentive to danger, God usually reveals to us the opportunity.

KIM: I've interviewed two congregations for the Toward Vitality research project who experienced the crisis of fire that destroyed their church buildings. In the midst of the grief of losing their buildings (often accompanied by a huge power struggle within congregations), both of these congregations took the time to regroup in a season of prayer and discernment about the kind of church that God was calling them to be. One congregation, in Beaver Falls, Pennsylvania, three years following the fire, is just now starting to launch a new kind of ministry that puts them on the path of creative outreach that ministers to folks with addictions. The other church, in Palmyra, Pennsylvania, rebuilt their facility by dreaming about the possibilities of outreach in their community. Both congregations birthed exciting new ministries through crisis, and they used the urgency factor to listen to God and discern the possibilities of what might be. It is interesting to me that once these congregations overcame the initial shock of the crisis, they were more able to look creatively at other changes that developed—worship style, small group development, and community outreach.

PAUL: So God's surprise factor is to reveal opportunities in crises—to open up a way forward in the storms. Our strategic game-changer is twofold: (1) to stay prayerful, in a posture of watchfulness for the windows of opportunity that open up, and (2) to seize those opportunities and to embrace certain crises as a way of fanning the urgency for the changes that are needed.

[I]t was now quite late in the day—they interrupted: "We are a long way out in the country, and it's very late. Pronounce a benediction and send these folks off so they can get some supper."

Jesus said, "You do it. Fix supper for them."

They replied, "Are you serious? You want us to go spend a fortune on food for their supper?"

But he was quite serious. "How many loaves of bread do you have? Take an inventory."

That didn't take long. "Five," they said, "plus two fish."

Jesus got them all to sit down in groups of fifty or a hundred—tthey looked like a patchwork quilt of wildflowers spread out on the green grass! He took the five loaves and two fish, lifted his face to heaven in prayer, blessed, broke, and gave the bread to the disciples, and the disciples in turn gave it to the people. He did the same with the fish. They all ate their fill. The disciples gathered twelve baskets of leftovers. (Mark 6:35-44 *THE MESSAGE*)

While he was still talking, some people came from the leader's house and told him, "Your daughter is dead. Why bother the Teacher any more?"

Jesus overheard what they were talking about and said to the leader, "Don't listen to them; just trust me."

He permitted no one to go in with him except Peter, James, and John. They entered the leader's house and pushed their way through the gossips looking for a story and neighbors bringing in casseroles. Jesus was abrupt: "Why all this busybody grief and gossip? This child isn't dead; she's sleeping." Provoked to sarcasm, they told him he didn't know what he was talking about.

...He clasped the girl's hand and said, *"Talitha koum,"* which means, "Little girl, get up." At that, she was up and walking around! This girl was twelve years of age. They, of course, were all beside themselves with joy. (Mark 5:35-42 *THE MESSAGE*)

Turning his impending doom into a sacramental event—on the day before he was executed—Jesus stamped meaning on his execution. He makes bad Friday good while it is still Thursday:

In the course of their meal, having taken and blessed the bread, he broke it and gave it to them. Then he said,

"Take, this is my body."

Taking the chalice, he gave it to them, thanking God, and they all drank from it. He said,

"This is my blood,

God's new covenant,

Poured out for many people.

"I'll not be drinking wine again until the new day when I drink it in the kingdom of God." (Mark 14:22-25 *THE MESSAGE*)

Five

COLLECT, DEVELOP, AND DEPLOY BRIGHT-EYED PEOPLE

KIM: *Quite a few years ago I was responsible for an after-school program for children at a large church in the Pittsburgh area. We had more than 150 children involved in small groups and a meal and choir rehearsal. I needed a team of bright-eyed people! I did not advertise from the pulpit or the newsletter for these folks—I went looking for them. I started with the parents of some of the kids that I already knew and asked them to point me to others. I partnered folks together to team-teach each class and used folks who were not interested in teaching to be the "class mover" who would get each group to their next place. That person's job was to just be there for the kids! There were also music people and meal people.*

Within a few weeks I had more than thirty people who were ready to work! I provided training and encouragement for each one. During the years that I directed this program, we had no dropouts among the staff, and we had tons of creative and energetic experiences that ended each year with a full-production musical! My job as director of the program was so easy (I'm almost embarrassed by this) because I had the right people doing the right jobs. A group of highly motivated folks who are empowered to be in ministry is an awesome experience for everyone!

PAUL: I love bright-eyed people. Without them, I would never have accomplished much in life. The search for and collection of bright-eyed people has been a centerpiece of my years as a pastor. It is also a centerpiece of my strategy work with pastors, especially those who take on very challenging, long-declining congregations.

KIM: I, too, love bright-eyed people! Some people have a certain energy that just radiates from them. They are inquisitive and eager and fun and passionate and busy and open and a gift to whatever group to which they belong! A few sentences of conversation and their eyes light up, showing genuine interest in you and whatever it is you are talking about! And when you hit on their area of interest and passion—watch out! They will just about explode out of their skin!

PAUL: Sometimes, only a handful of "bright eyes" are present in the congregation, and you have to go beyond the church walls to find enough of them to do anything. I have never gotten too scientific with this. I just know them when I see them, and in a church needing new life, I am on the watch for them! When a leader walks into a room and casts a vision of what could be, some eyes light up. Others don't. That is a pretty strong clue. I assume that most people will light up to certain leaders and possibilities and not light up in other contexts.

A few folks, by personality, are just enthusiastic and ready to go, in season and out. I think of Joanne in Gulf Breeze, Florida, in the 1990s. She met me in the hall the first time I walked in the doors of Gulf Breeze United Methodist Church and stayed in the middle of the action for years, until she and her husband retired in another city, only to light up a church there. The Joannes are rare. Now, some folks just like to hover near the action, a bit prone to mischief, busybodies. One can usually work with them, carefully. But Joanne had a true servant's heart, and I have not seen many miracles unfold without people like her in the mix!

Do you know a Joanne or two, Kim?

KIM: I certainly do. Both of our church-plant projects attracted bright-eyed people who helped us grow new congregations. In our early ministry, when we were bringing new life to existing congregations, there were many bright-eyed folks who were already there or appeared quickly to do a new thing.

PAUL: You know I should clarify that for the majority of the bright-eyed folks I have known, I just caught them at the right time and place in life. And the Holy Spirit showed up at that same time and place. There have been quite a few of them, and, like Joanne, they were all game-changers. They became key ministry catalysts as amazing things were accomplished in a variety of places. In almost every case, from the moment I bumped into them, they were in the game! Sort of like when Jesus met strangers and said, "Follow me," and people actually did! It wasn't that they followed me—in a couple cases I was not even the pastor—but a new ministry initiative just hit them and me at a point that we were ready to go somewhere new with God. And so we followed together!

A bright-eyed person named Jen wandered into a church that I work with in Portland, Maine, with deep suspicions. Yet according to the pastors, she immediately became a pivotal source of positive energy in that place, a key instigator for several initiatives. The following is from Jen's blog the week after she first wandered into the church where God would hook her:

So, I went to this church that meets in a space called Hope.Gate. Way...it's located in the lower level of a parking garage. (Yes, really.) Needless to say, I was dubious...more so because I was expecting something "new-agey" or fundamentalist than because of the location (which, as it turns out, is a lovely, warm, art-filled space without a concrete barricade in sight!)

What I found instead was a wonderful, welcoming group of people as diverse as the neighborhood in which Hope.Gate.Way is located. More important, I found a faith community that EN-COURAGES questions, even the most profound questions about God and Jesus and faith itself. And, within myself, I discovered how much I had missed (without realizing it) the spiritual connection that can only come from worshipping with others, no matter how much I was convinced that my personal relationship with God was enough.

I know that all of this is going to sound strange (at best) to some of you reading this, but my experience last week was transformative. I can't really explain what changed inside me, but I can feel it. I didn't realize how much I craved a spiritual home, a comfortable, safe place to celebrate my own faith while working through my ongoing questions about what it means to love God. I didn't realize I was envious of my sister, who had this life-changing feeling at a much younger age....

I have no idea what kind of impact this will ultimately have on my life...all I know is that I can feel a lightness in my heart that wasn't there a week ago, and that can only be a good thing. (http://jendimond.blogspot.com/2010/03/spiritual-but-not-religious.html)

KIM: Wow! This is a great testimony, Paul! We've experienced several of these transformational moments with folks when the lights just come on!

Sometimes we make the mistake of thinking that only extroverts are bright-eyed, but I have discovered that introverts can be just as bright-eyed and passionate! The difference really is in where they get their energy to be bright-eyed. My husband, Gary, is the extrovert. He needs to be with people in order to get energy. He's almost always the last person to leave a party, and the energy he gains from this experience can get him through days of being alone!

PAUL: Oh. I just thought he was the last out the door the other day because he liked my sangria.

KIM: Too funny, Paul! I, however, am an introvert. And while I enjoy people and gatherings, I get my energy from the downtime in my life. I have worked at week-long training events where I am teaching, listening, and interacting with folks from sunup to sundown. Usually by day three, I need to get away—just for a few hours—so I can recharge! I think it is safe to say that we are both bright-eyed people!

In order to help an existing congregation become a vital congregation you need to gather the bright-eyed people. Everyone knows the metaphor of the burning embers—they need to be working together in order to keep the fire bright!

My husband is a firebug. Whenever we have a small fire in the pit on our patio, he keeps his tools handy so that he can rearrange the logs to keep a fire burning as brightly as possible for as long as possible. In fact, he arranges the logs carefully before he even lights it, then he keeps the right amount of oxygen and new wood to keep it lit. Then he hovers over the fire so carefully. It is hysterical to watch.

PAUL: That is a great picture of what you do with bright-eyed people in a congregation!

But, Kim, I have seen more than a few churches where the embers were pretty few and far between. It can be hard to start a fire in some places.

KIM: It really depends on how low your congregation has become as to whether those bright-eyed people are still available. In many churches the bright-eyes have already left; and in that case you may need to stoke a few fires to bring them back or to reenergize those whose eyes have dimmed! One way for a pastor to start this search is observing the next church meeting. Who is paying attention? Who is taking notes? Who is adding to the conversation? These are your bright-eyed folks!

Last year I attended a council meeting of a church that had experienced a pastoral change in the midst of a transformation process, before the changes had solidified. They were in a bad place to begin with, and then the pastoral change seemed to send them right back to the pits again. At that meeting, no one looked up from their papers. Even those who spoke kept their heads down and talked to the floor. Fortunately, their new pastor had bright eyes, and his fire is now relighting some embers.

It amazes me that when a good change is coming, the bright-eyed folks usually start to appear. They may have been there all along, but they are almost always ready to do what is necessary to help something good happen!

PAUL: This has been my experience in every place. A few chapters ahead, in chapter 10, we will explore the case of Pastor Brad, casting vision in a new pastoral assignment, with an exuberance that is magnetic for bright-eyed people. When the right vision comes along, they may just appear out of the woodwork!

KIM: It can be tricky to recognize these people because sometimes they are obnoxious at first, until you can figure out a common ground for working together.

At one church, a young man, Chris, was always the first one to speak out on nearly every subject. Chris was loud and emotional and always present at meetings. The reaction of most of the other leaders was to turn away and try to ignore him. His manner took me aback until I started listening. Then I realized that he was a bright-eyed guy that needed to have a voice within this congregation. In the course of my time with that church, I was able to meet with Chris and encourage him to hang in there until we got the rest of the leaders to step up to his level of enthusiasm for what was happening. It wasn't long before he didn't seem so brash, because his enthusiasm caught on to fire up the whole team!

I can also show you another church that is having the opposite effect on their bright-eyed folks. They won't encourage them and won't empower them, and they are unknowingly letting them go to find other congregations where they can serve God.

PAUL: It makes us each want to stop and ask, "What kind of congregation is mine?"

As you discovered, enthusiastic Chris may require a little coaching. He has positive energy, but he is also functioning in a system that is not used to his energy or his style. There is nothing wrong with taking him onto the sidelines to make clear that he is a key ally, bringing something valuable to the table, yet to share that we need to think as a team as we advance new ideas and execute them. That may seem like a potentially awkward conversation, but it actually is a case of taking Chris very seriously and empowering him to be a part of the team. And people usually appreciate being taken seriously.

KIM: It is not always easy to empower people. First, we have to find the people we want to empower! The right people have to be connected with the right tasks. Many churches use some system of recruitment to find leaders and plug them into existing positions—defined by the denomination or an organizational chart. Usually many of the jobs are committee-oriented, focused on making decisions for the church, or team-oriented around standardized programs offered by the church. Often these are static jobs that just stay the same year after year.

PAUL: It is sort of like running a department store for which the national headquarters office ships you a preset array of sizes and styles. With real department stores, of course, after the popular items are gone, the less popular sizes and ugly sweaters go on clearance sale, while new more appealing merchandise comes in, until almost everybody can find something to wear that fits their size and style. But imagine that the store simply handed out the clothing items every year at an annual gathering, calling people down to the front of the room by name. "Sue Smith. Wear this for the next year. Somebody has to wear it. And it seems to us you are as good as anyone else." Would that be nuts or what? "Yes, we know it is two sizes too big, but do the best you can with it. The woman who wore it last year only wore it a couple times anyway."

This is the way many churches assign jobs and ministry tasks to their people.

KIM: And there are always a few important jobs that somebody has to "wear."

PAUL: Sure, finances have to be managed. Building and property issues also must be managed. And every church needs somebody or a team that works alongside the pastor to oversee personnel policy, hiring, salaries, and so on. But some churches organize so as to keep those kinds of jobs to an efficient minimum because they want to free up as many people as possible to work where their gifts and calling are aligned with need.

A lot of bright-eyed folks are wasted in tasks that are ill suited to their gifts or that are just unnecessary in the first place. In late 2009, I spent a week embedded in the life of one of the fastest-growing churches in the United States, just to study what was going on, to see what was in the water. Christ the King Community Church is based in Burlington, Washington. Their pastor, Dave Browning, wrote a book entitled *Deliberate Simplicity*. If there is a simple way to get a job done, they find it. This church came to the conviction that we make many church tasks more complex than is truly necessary, and along the way we spend a lot of unnecessary money as well. Because they found ways to get the church chores done with as few folks as possible in as simple a way as possible, most of the people were left with time and energy to take on ministry tasks and dreams that caused their eyes to light up, and that had an impact in the communities where they had campuses.

KIM: Rather than just filling slots, it sounds as if they were focused on mobilizing ministry leaders!

PAUL: Exactly.

KIM: Mobilizing allows us to empower people by recognizing their God-given abilities and passion. Then we can get them doing what it is they are most able to do. This in turn fuels further passion and energy for ministry.

PAUL: How can churches make the shift from simply filling lots of slots to mobilizing leaders?

KIM: I think the most important first step in mobilizing is for the pastor and existing leaders to intentionally pay attention to the people around them! This means getting to know folks through conversation and relationship. Discover what folks are passionate about! Only by listening and getting to know people can we truly help make good ministry connections.

PAUL: And then we can also help people with similar interests and dreams to find one another.

KIM: My friend Nick is passionate about hunger ministries. Do you think it is a good idea to recruit him for the building maintenance team? People have limited time, but when we help connect them to ministries that are fun for them, *they will spend more time and do a better job.*

PAUL: I really believe in that last point!

KIM: There are folks in your congregation who are suited to and passionate about fixing leaky pipes and chairing various committees, but it is only through relationship and interaction with folks that we can know this!

PAUL: There are young retirees who bound out of bed each morning, enlivened by the thought that they could spend the day puttering around the church building, fixing things! Others have managerial wisdom and a knack for leading committees to make great decisions, efficiently.

KIM: If my friend Nick has a passion for seeing that everyone has access to fresh food, then we should do all that we can to keep his time free from tedious committee meetings, so that he will have capacity for the things that will bring him (and others) the most joy. We need to leave Nick to glean for Society for St. Andrew or participate in a food co-op.

PAUL: One of the biggest dysfunctions I see in traditional churches is the belief that we need to get as many people as possible involved in making decisions. So we take work that could be accomplished with two dozen people on a few teams and pass out scores of committee positions. Half the committees never meet. And those that do, seldom make a really significant decision. So people stop attending the meetings out of sheer boredom. Then when the church tries to consolidate the work for efficiency's sake, there is often a group of laity that cries, "Foul!" because they see less representation in the decision-making bodies. This is almost always related to control issues. It is somewhat rare for newer members to worry about how many people are deployed in decision making. Most of the new people will have little interest in committee work; they would rather be deployed where ministry happens, where the results are experienced and blessings go around.

KIM: When Gary and I were planting a church in western Pennsylvania, it was my job to get the children's ministry started. My vision for this ministry was to get as many people involved executing small parts of the ministry until we had some experience together and really discovered what it was we needed to do. I watched folks interact with their own children and with other people's children. I had conversations with folks about what our children's ministry could look like. I paid attention when people's eyes lit up, realizing that certain folks were more able and ready to see the possibilities.

PAUL: And I assume that you took bright eyes as a green light to invite them to help out.

KIM: That was it. And before long we had a great Sunday morning children's ministry with lots of adults having fun interacting with lots of kids!

Two things we have to figure out are, first, how can we effectively do what we need to do, and second, who is most likely to have the gifts and abilities to get us there?

PAUL: Would you say that it would be helpful for a church to step back and think about its mission and then ask, "How can we live out this mission in our context?"

KIM: Yes! A lot of churches are fuzzy on their missions, but many are fairly clear. For example, the mission of The United Methodist Church is "to make disciples of Jesus Christ for the transformation of the world." In that particular denomination, even if a congregation has not done the work of creating a local mission statement, they already have a good starting place.

Your church may frame its mission slightly differently, but whatever your mission is, that becomes the ruler for evaluating what you do. An effective way for a United Methodist church to decide on the validity of any church activity is to put it alongside the measure of making disciples. Evaluate every activity that can be evaluated with this question: how did that help us make disciples for Jesus Christ so that we can change the world? Study groups, mission trips, fund-raisers, worship, youth ministry, everything! If the activity isn't helping you make disciples, then that is a good indicator that it isn't something in which you should be investing time and energy and especially resources. You may need to start, of course, with defining what your congregation, in your context, means by "making disciples." Sometimes we assume we know what that means when we really don't, so a simple, defined statement might help everyone get on the same page!

PAUL: In my years at Gulf Breeze Church, we framed our mission by three movements: hospitality, hope, and healing—our definition of what it meant to be a disciple of Jesus. We measured everything we did in terms of those three movements—all three movements at every level of church life. If, for example, an activity did not intentionally relate to healing, toward the redemption and transformation of human life, then we would conclude that we could better spend our time on something else.

If you wonder how well aligned your church is between your stated purpose and your actual behavior, the *Readiness 360* inventory offers a great tool for any church to assess this (www.readiness360.org).

KIM: Aaron is the associate pastor of a church in the process of aligning their ministries with their stated mission focus. Aaron told me that in one arm he carries the new focus for ministry and in the other arm he lovingly holds the persons and ministries who will be stretched and possibly frustrated by the need to conform all things to a more focused cause. Aaron is thinking both pastorally and strategically. He is banking on good relational equity because he really does love the people! He is seeking to lead this church to be better at what they do, without damaging the people who are attached to those ministries where change is coming. In the midst of this story, I also remember Jesus' stories about pruning and the benefit of a well-tended vineyard!

PAUL: Sometimes when ministry is being pruned and reframed, and people are displaced from the tasks and jobs they have had for years, an opportunity can arise to steer them toward a new fun thing—and one hopefully in keeping with the focus of the church's ministry—or possibly an opportunity to steer them toward a ministry or cause beyond church out in the community. I also have observed that when a church has an *everyone-in-ministry* philosophy, it is easier to redirect people occasionally when old ministries wind down or morph into something new.

KIM: Here is another opportunity to coach people using those questions from chapter 2. A specific conversation about redirecting folks to other ministries is an important part of this step. Many thriving churches today have clear expectations that members will be involved serving others.

PAUL: And a few churches will also specify that they want all of the people serving in some capacity *beyond* church projects and ministries!

KIM: A disciple is one who worships, learns, gives, welcomes, and serves. A large part of mobilizing leaders and servants in ministry is simply letting everyone know that this is a part of what is expected, instead of just assuming that it will happen! There are lots of resources on the market today to help people learn their spiritual gifts and understand how God can use each person to have an impact within his or her circle of influence. We simply need to expect that folks will do this!

PAUL: If this is a new concept for your church—the idea that membership has responsibilities—then I say give it some time. Introduce it in stages. Expect to take four to six years for some folks to change paradigms. Some people will not really hear that you are challenging them to get into ministry until they have experienced four or more cycles of annual emphasis and teaching and mobilization to get everyone into ministry. But eventually most of the late adapters will come around.

KIM: Clear job descriptions, task descriptions, coaches, and, where possible, mentors can make all the difference between a person having a great time accepting a volunteer service opportunity at church and that person having a miserable time. I often suggest that we be proactive by making sure that every role or responsibility be handled by two people: one who knows the job and one who is learning the job. I alluded to this practice in the chapter about loving one another, so this shouldn't be a shock to you! When I was putting together children's ministry teams, it was so much easier to partner people to work together than to expect one teacher to do everything in a classroom. If you can give specific tasks to people and provide them with mentors who will support them as they learn, this is a win for the next generation of leaders and servants and also a win for the overall congregation!

PAUL: In terms of mentoring, sometimes it is appropriate to show new folks how you approach a task and then to let them assess if they wish to continue in the same approach or change it a bit. For several years, my teenage son brewed coffee on Sunday mornings for about 1,500 people. He made the coffee in a gigantic commercial machine. There was a right way and a wrong way to make the coffee; not much to debate or change, short of getting a different coffee machine. But in other kinds of tasks—say leading a small group—we can share tips, and there may be a few things that need to happen each time a group meets. Each leader will approach the task a bit differently, however, and this is appropriate.

KIM: Yes, and sometimes in figuring out their way forward, new leaders experience some failures along the way.

PAUL: I have failed at just about every task I have ever tried at least once, and a few twice. But I seldom fail three times. If you will stay off my back and stay in supportive relationship with me, I tend to get it right eventually or find my way to a more constructive ministry role. I'm not an idiot. Most people are not. Give us a chance to learn what we are doing, and we may knock your socks off.

KIM: Remember when Jesus' disciples came back from their two-by-two exercise to admit that they couldn't cast out every demon or heal every disease? Jesus didn't scold them; he gently told them that they needed to increase their prayer and fasting (see, for example, Mark 9:14-29)!

PAUL: Perfect. Tell me what I can do to improve my performance. That's constructive.

In the early stage of a church transformation, so much hinges on collecting these bright-eyed folks. We really need to hunt for them. Build relationship with them. Gather them. Keep in touch with them. Introduce them to one another. Play with them. Pray for them. Invest time in them. Allow them to keep you energized. If there is any one statistic that is important to manage and grow in the early phase of a transformation project, it is the number of bright eyes! If you have only three people, seek to double that three to six this year. If you have a dozen, seek to find a dozen more. *I'll tell you, Kim: if a church is gaining bright-eyed people steadily, any decline can be arrested, and any church can begin to grow and thrive again.* I tell pastors to keep a list of these folks in their top desk drawer.

KIM: And pray over that list every day!

PAUL: Seriously!

KIM: If we are having a hard time identifying the bright eyes, then we should pray that God will send us some! Ask God to send us people who will partner with us to bring the change needed to create a vital congregation that will impact the community for God's kingdom! Then we must make sure to keep our own eyes bright so that we can find those whom God sends!

God's surprise comes by providing the bright-eyed folks for the work!

Here are five strategic responses we can use to get bright-eyed folks involved in ministry:

• Look for them intentionally—collect them, if you will.

• Discover their passions and tie those passions to ministry opportunities.

• Lift up an awareness of the value of everyone in ministry.

• Give new servant leaders coaching or mentoring.

• Encourage folks gently, even when they fail.

PAUL: I have never done this before, but I am going to offer a money-back guarantee. If anyone reading this book will keep a list of bright-eyed people and seek to double that list for three years—for example, you have six to start, then six becomes twelve, twelve becomes twenty-four, and twenty-four becomes forty-eight—and keep a record of that, with names attached and her or his church does not begin to grow numerically in worship attendance, she or he can contact me, and I will reimburse the price paid for this book out of my pocket. (You can contact me at epicentergroup.dc@gmail.com.)

KIM: You sound as if you believe in this.

PAUL: I totally believe in this. I know that bright-eyed people change the game.

> He noticed two boats tied up. The fishermen had just left them and were out scrubbing their nets. He climbed into the boat that was Simon's and asked him to put out a little from the shore. Sitting there, using the boat for a pulpit, he taught the crowd.
>
> When he finished teaching, he said to Simon, "Push out into deep water and let your nets out for a catch."
>
> Simon said, "Master, we've been fishing hard all night and haven't caught even a minnow. But if you say so, I'll let out the nets." It was no sooner said than done—a huge haul of fish, straining the nets past capacity. They waved to their partners in the other boat to come help them. They filled both boats, nearly swamping them with the catch.

Simon Peter, when he saw it, fell to his knees before Jesus. "Master, leave. I'm a sinner and can't handle this holiness. Leave me to myself." When they pulled in that catch of fish, awe overwhelmed Simon and everyone with him. It was the same with James and John, Zebedee's sons, coworkers with Simon.

...They pulled their boats up on the beach, left them, nets and all, and followed him. (Luke 5:2-11 *THE MESSAGE*)

He climbed a mountain and invited those he wanted with him. They climbed together. He settled on twelve, and designated them apostles. The plan was that they would be with him, and he would send them out to proclaim the Word and give them authority to banish demons. (Mark 3:13-15 *THE MESSAGE*)

He sent them off with these instructions:

"Don't think you need a lot of extra equipment for this. *You* are the equipment. No special appeals for funds. Keep it simple.

"And no luxury inns. Get a modest place and be content there until you leave.

"If you're not welcomed, not listened to, quietly withdraw. Don't make a scene. Shrug your shoulders and be on your way."

Then they were on the road. They preached with joyful urgency that life can be radically different; right and left they sent the demons packing; they brought wellness to the sick, anointing their bodies, healing their spirits. (Mark 6:8-13 *THE MESSAGE*)

MAKE A FEW HELPFUL, BOLD MOVES[1]

When Sheila arrived at Cornerstone Church, they were overspending their income by about $4,000 per month and eating up their building fund in the process just paying operating expenses. Fourteen months remained before the Day of Reckoning when they would run out of money. They were already $40,000 in debt to their building fund. Negative emotions dominated church life, with complaints about everything from how much the preacher was paid to whether we needed such toilet paper in the men's room. Meetings were not pretty. The church had a budget that was entirely out of touch with actual income, so the church treasurer had become the de facto budget—in human form—determining what bills the church should pay and what bills they should not. Sheila realized that nothing good was going to happen at Cornerstone until they stopped the financial bleed. There was no point in waiting a year. She did not want a study committee. She simply wanted to balance income and spending. Now.

Sheila convened key leaders and made her recommendations. These included laying off the associate pastor and taking the remaining two people to half their current hours, if they would stay. The associate pastor had been a thorn in the side of the last pastor. As Sheila solved one problem, she dealt with another. The following board meeting, at which the cuts were confirmed, was horrendous by all accounts. They said Sheila's honeymoon was over in her fifth week on the job. Some

71

people called her the devil. Attendance was down 20 percent the following Sunday, but income was actually up. The congregational singing and after-worship coffee hour seemed more robust than usual. The church was free from the burden of financial chaos. Sheila preached an upbeat and hopeful sermon. A new day had dawned at Cornerstone.

A year later, attendance was up by 30 percent, and income up by about $3,500 a month, almost to the place where they could have afforded the old budget. But as new spending was instituted, it went to new places. (A set amount each month even went to pay back the building fund for funds borrowed, not a lot, but enough to state to potential donors that the church would handle their building fund gifts with integrity.)

Cornerstone had pruned their old branches, and now new branches were able to grow. Two new part-time staff positions were added, with different assortments of responsibilities and focuses. Church meetings were much more relaxed, punctuated with laughter and joy. And whenever the church treasurer tried to play God with the money, Sheila would simply ask her, "Is it in the budget?" "Did we vote on this budget?" "Is our income in line with this budget?" When all three answers were yes, then Sheila would look at the treasurer with a smile and a sparkle in her eye and say, "Well then, I suggest you write the check."

The demon of financial pandemonium had been exorcised from Cornerstone. And the church's newfound health showed in almost every setting.

PAUL: It is not always a matter of money, but in Sheila's case, she tackled the money problem, the morale problem, and the dysfunctional staff problem in one play. It was the game-changer she needed to start a productive pastorate.

I first learned about the meaning of *game-changer* at the Cotton Bowl on New Year's Day 1981, when Baylor played Alabama. I was a student at Baylor. We held Bear Bryant's team to zero during the first half, and we were elated! We had scored a touchback, making the halftime score 2–0 Baylor. But Bryant and his coaching staff had cracked the code on Baylor's strategy during the second quarter. It was complicated enough that they could not effectively respond on the sidelines. They needed to take their players to the locker room and teach them what Baylor was doing and how to respond appropriately. The game changed. Alabama proceeded to score forty points in the second half. Baylor's score remained two. Honestly, I don't know enough about the subtleties of football strategy to catch all that Alabama started doing differently after halftime. But they made a few key changes, and everything shifted.

KIM: There are all sorts of game-changers within congregations—new pastor, death of a matriarch/patriarch, big givers move away, and even life catastrophes for individuals and communities—and all of these crises can be life giving. The recent recession has been a big game-changer for many congregations. Many of the game-changers are opportunities for us to be courageous in our attitudes toward the future!

PAUL: Definitely! But if you can't find a game-changer, the next best thing would be simply to fix something big.

KIM: I've known some pastors who have developed a reputation for creating chaos when none existed, just to provide an opportunity to change or fix something!

PAUL: Creating a little chaos may be just the thing to help identify what really needs fixing! It may not be anything strategic, but it could be something that has been nagging the church for too long. Show people that you can fix something and move on. This is good for the credibility of the new leadership, and it is good for the church's morale and momentum.

Kim, why do you think churches develop inertia? How do we get stuck?

KIM: Let's be honest, Paul: most people really want to be contented and happy. Most of the time that happens only when we don't rock the boat and everything moves along quietly. Too often, it's just easier to look past the things that need fixing and to sweep problems under the rug. I often warn congregations that they could die of "terminal niceness"—that tendency to avoid working on the hard stuff because it might hurt someone's feelings. Remember what Jesus did when he saw the moneychangers in the temple? He cleaned it out, made his point, and moved on!

PAUL: And that took nerve. Ed Friedman, the brilliant Jewish pastoral theologian, wrote a book that many of our readers know and love, *Generation to Generation*. It's a classic. Friedman's last book, written just prior to his death, is far less known. *A Failure of Nerve* is pointed at leaders in established faith communities who can't find the wherewithal to stand up for anything risky. Every church needs some leaders—lay and clergy—who will rise to the occasion and lead! Take some heat, but take a stand, and go!

KIM: I've noticed throughout our Toward Vitality research that the game-changer in many situations is the arrival of a pastor who is not afraid to lead. The effectiveness of the change seems to be tied to how quickly the laypeople catch up to the leader and join in on the new direction.

PAUL: A couple of winters ago, we had a snow and ice storm in Washington. It hit at rush hour like a summer thunderstorm, roaring and dumping up to nine inches of wet sludgy snow on commuters within a short time. Some people did not get home from their fifteen-mile commute until 5:30 the next morning. As I think about group inertia and how it works, I ponder that traffic fiasco. What I know is this:

- Most people's cars were perfectly able to drive, even in the muck.

- A heavy rain earlier in the day totally washed away all salt and road treatments, setting up a perfect storm.

- Many city buses and eighteen-wheeler trucks had trouble. About seventy buses got stuck along with untold commercial trucks, usually sliding sideways and blocking a major traffic artery for a couple of hours.

- Only a few hundred cars in a metro area of five million souls had trouble or eventually ran out of gas. But every time a car got stuck, thousands more stopped.

- To save gasoline in a commute where some cars did not move for two and three hours at a time, many people turned off their engines. This saved gas, but it greatly increased the time it took for drivers to respond to any opportunity to move. A few drivers fell asleep! Rather than all moving forward in quick response to the next, each car had to start its engine before it could move or hop out to wake up the driver in front of them! This lack of readiness to move probably doubled the time that it took for folks to drive the George Washington Parkway to the Beltway.

• People were greatly distressed—miserable about the situation, all very hungry, some becoming angry, some panicking (due to nursing infants or other persons needing them a few miles and a few hours away), and many embarrassed by having to relieve themselves in front of God and a hundred other motorists.

I listened to the ten o'clock news that night and learned, from the warmth of my downtown home, about the disaster that was unfolding all over the region. I had no idea until then what was going on. The news anchor got the Maryland Secretary of Transportation on the phone and righteously demanded, "Ms. Secretary, what are you going to do about this?" This was actually a bit of unnecessary TV drama—I mean what is a state secretary of transportation supposed to do exactly at this point? Fly a helicopter in and rescue a million drivers? Tow trucks and highway patrol cars could not get through to help anyone. It was really a conundrum. As it turned out, there were some bold, helpful actions that improved the situation, allowing people to get home:

• Abandoned cars were pushed off into the woods (or worse), without much regard for dings and damage. Motorists themselves accomplished some of this work.

• Local helping agencies ordered all their people to report to work; it became an *all-hands-on-deck* moment.

• Motorists took initiative to leave the roadway and cut new trails and exits off the controlled access roads, without regard for private property or normal traffic laws.

• In some areas, both sides of the street began to flow traffic in a single direction away from the city center, although this was not possible in many places due to complex commuting patterns.

• Officials closed access points to some roads in order to force folks onto alternative routes, helping them avoid the worst points of gridlock in the region and get home faster.

The entire situation lasted about thirteen hours. Some systems experience similar inertia for thirteen or more years! It is important that new leaders, not yet inebriated with the local inertia, take immediate and sometimes extreme action to fix the problems. Some situations are so obviously broken that waiting is just not helpful.

KIM: What a dramatic example of inertia and boldness. We had some similar situations where we lived last winter, but it's a much smaller city, so the logjam didn't last so long! I hope something was learned through this experience that will make a difference in the next storm.

This topic—the opportunity for bold moves—offers us the chance to pull together everything else that we've been talking about.

- Where are we experiencing love, both inside and outside the congregation?

- What is most urgent?

- What does God have to say about our situation?

- Who are the bright-eyed people who can motivate a bold move?

I have been coaching Andy over the past year. One of Andy's key goals has been to listen for a word from God! For several months we talked about listening and keeping a journal and what gets in the way of hearing. Then one evening, God spoke through a *60 Minutes* episode about homeless children and the difficulty of finding shelter since most don't accept families. During the broadcast, Andy recognized the place of the interview as his own daughter's school cafeteria! God showed Andy a significant human need in his own backyard. Andy already had a relationship with the school principal, and he knew a nearby hotel manager who sometimes helped their church host persons in crisis. Andy also had a church full of people with resources, although he would say that a lot of these resources were at the time unknown and dormant.

PAUL: And Andy was now in a position to lead. He was able to help connect all of the above in true community.

KIM: Within ten days, carloads of food and clothes were headed to the hotel where a food and clothing bank was created. Rooms were purchased in bulk and made available for homeless families, although they weren't totally paid for by the church. The school principal connected families to Andy and to the hotel. The church responded wholeheartedly to this need of which many folks were simply not aware. During a special "Fast for Food" campaign during Lent, $17,000 was collected for this need—unprecedented in this congregation. Small teams were created to build relationships with the folks who were housed at the hotel.

PAUL: So I am wondering how this bold new mission affected the congregation. I can only assume that the church discovered new energy for life.

KIM: Andy reported three things that happened within the life of this congregation. (1) There was an awakening to the reality that a practical need for the church existed in their community. (2) *Mission* was redefined as something that happens in our backyard, rather than overseas. There were many "Oh, I can help with that" moments, which helped people take the first steps into action. (3) The church discovered a confidence that they could make a difference in the world.

Andy still struggles and deals with church people who just "don't get it." He's learning to bless them anyway and keep moving forward!*

PAUL: In the last few years, I worked as part of a team planting a new faith community in downtown Washington DC, in partnership with a 200-year-old congregation. Both our new community (Sunday Night @ Foundry) and the larger community (Foundry United Methodist Church) are thriving. Our church has been growing larger, younger, and browner with each passing year.

In recent months, a sequence of gigantic projects have captured us, captivated us, energized us, and rallied us. These bold commitments toward blessing and transforming our community are in fact transforming us in magnificent ways. To borrow from Jim Collins's language, they each related to "big, hairy, audacious goals" (see chapter 5 in *Built to Last* [New York: Harper Collins, 2002]). But they are not simply related to building our church for its own sake. These commitments range from ending chronic homelessness in our city within a few years, to banding in solidarity with day laborers and

*Thanks to Andy Searles for permission to use his story.

new immigrants, to creating a church that is a snapshot of our neighborhood both ethnically and socioeconomically, to forming a long-term partnership with sisters and brothers in Haiti. And others. We are making measurable progress on all fronts. And most of our new members are signing on because they share at least one of these passions.

In the early season of transformation work, you don't need six bold commitments. One is fine. Two is plenty. But choose projects and social values that are rooted in your church's understanding of the gospel, projects that will function to rally the energy and passion of the members and your neighbors. Pick something big—big enough that it feels impossible on your own, but inspirational enough that it rallies folks even from far beyond the church rolls to help!

The average age of people signing on with Foundry Church in DC is probably thirty-two years old. A good portion of our neighborhood is composed of international folks with an array of cultural and religious traditions. The vast majority of this neighborhood has no interest in organized Christian anything. And yet we have grown. Without Foundry's boldness, the church would probably be a shrinking, aging, isolated group in an increasingly decrepit building…and our new Sunday Night community would never have taken root. *

KIM: Paul, during the time we have written this book, I have attended a local church in the Nashville area. Edgehill United Methodist Church is a welcoming congregation (my first priority), and they have made room for me to begin to participate in their ministry. They actually know enough about the needs in their community to be able to identify which of those needs they can do something about! They know that this area—about sixteen blocks in an impoverished neighborhood—does not have a decent grocery store that sells healthy foods. They know that there is a violence problem. They know that there are many single-teenage-parent families. And they also know that folks are transient and have a difficult time finding and affording the "stuff" of life. While some of these problems are just too big right now, this community is boldly addressing one of them. Edgehill is working to develop a free store that will allow the whole community a place to share "stuff." The ministry part of the free store is that it becomes a place to build relationships. Church folks are trained to remember that hospitality and conversation are a big part of the shopping experience!*

*Thanks to Edgehill and Foundry United Methodist Churches for permission to share their stories.

PAUL: And, I might add, these outwardly focused ministries helped hook you as a new member. They hooked you, and you didn't need more stuff in your life. I have worked with a church this year—the average age of members is late seventies—that decided to focus energy on loving folks in an assisted living center and a nursing home. And now they have attracted younger new members who will not need assisted living services for decades! They hooked them because they rolled up their sleeves and boldly did something with their faith!

This is one of the key ways that Jesus hooked people as well! He was announcing the kingdom of God, for crying out loud, breaking into this world and into the current Roman regime and status quo. His ministry started when he publicly identified with John's movement in the desert, just before they came to arrest and execute John. He had nerve from the get-go! And then Jesus lived into the new reality he was announcing: with healing; with the crossing of social boundaries; with clear defiance of certain practices, phobias, and habits within his own faith community in order to call people to a higher vision, a superior ethic, and a better world. *Bold* was Jesus' middle name. And it made his movement very sticky!

There was something much stickier for you about Edgehill than if you had discovered simply a cute annual craft sale.

KIM: You got that right. This is a church that cares for its community—the people in the neighborhood.

Most congregational leaders probably already know a few bold moves that their congregation could be taking. God is already stirring the hearts and minds of somebody within any given congregation. You can count on that. Often what is lacking is the courage to take action! Here we go back to the fear thing: What will others say? How will the "money" people respond? What about our older folks who, together, often provide the most financial support? What if this fails, then what?

PAUL: Listen for the passion and the stirring that is real and present in the lives of a few folks. Get them into a room together. Encourage them to talk out their dreams with some folks who are experts in whatever field is relevant to those dreams—usually experts from beyond the congregation, but who carry the knowledge we require in order to understand the need and succeed in our attempts to be helpful. Wait until you can find at least five people willing to own the project together as a first ministry team, then set them loose. In most cases, this will require no vote by any church committee. Let them get started. Let them tell the stories. In time, when their work grows, and they want to invite the whole church to invest money or time in a large way, then there may be a time officially to endorse their work, to give them a budget, or even to change church policies. But baby steps at first!

KIM: The surprise of God's involvement is often to open our minds to see and imagine bold and audacious acts that could serve to transform how the community sees our church and how we see ourselves. I've talked with many churches in recent months that have experienced this kind of opportunity, in which one or two folks get a great idea for an outward-focused ministry; they find a few others who share the passion, and usually, they are able to get the ministry started without any delay from committees!

PAUL: Our challenge is to step into the audacity—this is the action of a permission-giving church! Show some nerve!

Jesus knew right away what they were thinking, and said, "Why are you so skeptical? Which is simpler: to say to the paraplegic, 'I forgive your sins,' or say, 'Get up, take your stretcher, and start walking'? Well, just so it's clear that I'm the Son of Man and authorized to do either, or both..." (he looked now at the paraplegic), "Get up. Pick up your stretcher and go home." (Mark 2:8-11 *THE MESSAGE*)

One Sabbath day [Jesus] was walking through a field of ripe grain. As his disciples made a path, they pulled off heads of grain. The Pharisees told on them to Jesus: "Look, your disciples are breaking Sabbath rules!"

Jesus said, "Really? Haven't you ever read what David did when he was hungry, along with those who were with him? How he entered the sanctuary and ate fresh bread off the altar, with the Chief Priest Abiathar right there watching—holy bread that no one but priests were allowed to eat—and handed it out to his companions?" (Mark 2:23-26 *THE MESSAGE*)

They arrived at Jerusalem. Immediately on entering the Temple Jesus started throwing out everyone who had set up shop there, buying and selling. He kicked over the tables of the bankers and the stalls of the pigeon merchants. He didn't let anyone even carry a basket through the Temple. And then he taught them, quoting this text: "My house was designated a house of prayer for the nations; You've turned it into a hangout for thieves." (Mark 11:15-17 *THE MESSAGE*)

Seven

CREATE LEGEND ON THE COMMUNITY GRAPEVINE

No sooner had Laura arrived as the new pastor at First Church than she discovered that she would have to attend the city council meeting the next evening—her second night in town. The council would decide whether or not to pay retired public servants sixty cents on the dollar for their pension or to raise taxes so as to pay them fully what they were owed. For Laura this was a no-brainer. She had never been a political crusader, but this was a clear justice issue: would the city come together to honor its legal and moral commitments to its retired police officers, firefighters, and librarians or not? She took a deep breath and walked into city hall.

Laura introduced herself at the microphone—to the community and probably to some parishioners she had not met yet. She spoke calmly and lovingly, "These are the servants who have loved this community across many decades. They could have moved away, many of them, made more money—but they did not. Because they loved this town! They loved many of you. In some cases, they risked their lives for you. As of yesterday, I, too, am a citizen here. And if I need to pay more city taxes so that our city can do right by those who have given their lives to make this community what it is, then I for one am prepared to do that, and I expect all of us here to be prepared to do the right thing." The council tabled the pension cut,

83

they raised taxes the following week, and Laura became a legend before she had unpacked half her boxes or preached her first sermon. The legend: here is a pastor who cares about people and who has courage to stand and gracefully admonish the community to do the right thing.

PAUL: Every church has a reputation of some sort, a public perception. For some, it may be as simple as the church that waits too long to mow the grass or the church with the loud bells or the church where no one can recall a living human being ever walking in or out!

KIM: Every pastor also has a reputation of some sort—equally public. One may be the pastor who golfs in the low eighties, another might be the pastor who visits in the nursing home, and yet another is the pastor who stood up for the rights of marginalized people.

PAUL: In cases where the pastor and church are invisible to the community or missing in action, they may have a reputation of being irrelevant. (I could add that reputations are not always accurate, but they are powerful.)

KIM: Your point about reputations and accuracy is true. So many church reputations are built on one person's experience with just one other person, which may or may not be reflective of the whole congregation. A trustee's decision about who can use the church building can reflect badly if someone is denied use of the facilities for a wedding or funeral. I often wonder how much the reputation of the church was damaged in the 1960s and '70s when young people were spurned because of an unwanted pregnancy or drug issues or for living together outside marriage.

PAUL: Or in recent years, as young people see the church as the last major community institution protecting and encouraging homophobia. Often the first question that I am asked about my church by smart heterosexual young people in Washington DC is: "Does your church accept gay people?"

Back in my twenties, I was assigned as pastor to a church with financial problems. We cut a deal with a local café to move our midweek activities to the café, to save on utilities at the church building. They said that café business picked up at 7:00 p.m. on Wednesdays because the Methodist choir was rehearsing in the banquet room. At Raders Café, it was Lions Club on Mondays and Methodist Choir Practice on Wednesdays.

It was a small Texas town and apparently the townsfolk liked the music. Some of those folks grew up on such music but no longer attended church. They also said that the café stayed busier than usual at the 8:00 p.m. hour after choir practice, when different committees from our church would meet. The finance committee talked incessantly (and not too quietly) about how we were short of money. Trustees talked about the building falling in. And the church board, which met on every fourth Wednesday, discouraged by the previous two weeks of meetings, was an often cantankerous gathering. In fact, during the 8:00 p.m. hour on Wednesdays, diners would actually move to the side of the room where they could hear more clearly. Some would order another cup of coffee and peach cobbler and settle in for the weekly soap opera. We became well known for two things in that little town. We had a great choir, and we were always near financial Armageddon. If we had just called it a night with choir rehearsal, meeting at the diner could have been a good thing.

KIM: What a great story! It would be an interesting study for readers to talk to their friends and neighbors to find out what they think about a variety of churches in their community.

PAUL: Often a church, at the beginning of a transformation season, has some negative legend attached to it in the community. If not negative, the issue may be simply that the church is invisible. Community people may have stopped paying attention to the building or anything going on years ago. In either case, the sooner the church can create some positive community buzz, the better!

KIM: All the more reason to ask folks their opinion of our churches. Even if they have nothing to say, that is important information.

PAUL: …that our church is a big blank in their minds. Yes, that is important to know.

KIM: And knowing this can help us make the case for the transformation that is needed within the congregation!

PAUL: A couple of years ago, my church sent a group to a street in the church's neighborhood during our Sunday morning services. We found folks in the playground behind the church with their kids, in the dog parks, in front of Whole Foods, and in front of Starbucks. (The Starbucks people were happy to chat so long as we let them get their coffee first—never get between people and their first cup of coffee.) We learned a lot about how our church is perceived by our neighbors! This was extremely helpful to us as we planned a new outreach initiative.

KIM: There are so many ways that churches can create positive buzz!

PAUL: Oh my goodness, there certainly are! Just a quick list of possibilities:

- The church that gives away money in the offering one Sunday—$10s, $20s, and maybe even a couple of $50s or $100s—instructing the congregants to invest the money in serving the community. If you get a newspaper reporter to follow the whole process, she or he will have a boatload of feel-good stories when folks begin reporting what they did out in the neighborhood.

- The church that finds and adopts a single high-profile helping project in the community and then pours volunteer energy into that: flooding a local school with reading tutors or mentors or adopting a public housing project (in collaboration with residents and management) to help create landscaping, playgrounds, trash cleanup, and possible after-school programs for kids.

- The church that finds a group of people in the community who are being treated unfairly by a larger and more powerful system, and stands publicly with the folks who are being mistreated.

- The church that hits a home run with one of its regular programs (a children's ministry, a music ministry, a recovery ministry) and decides to take it up a notch and build its PR around that highly credible ministry.

- The church that adopts a nursing home and regularly visits the people whom no one visits (of course, in collaboration with the management).

- The church that takes its Christmas Eve service to the hospital auditorium, to make it available to families with hospitalized loved ones—possibly caroling in certain sections of the hospital after the service. (Did I mention, in collaboration with the management?)

- The church that partners with the hospital social worker to send a casserole and fresh salad home with each patient discharged from the hospital over a period of weeks.

- The church that builds a new children's playground—or a dog park for that matter—in the middle of the community, in co-operation with the city parks people, and with invitation to community residents to help.

- The church that sponsors a karaoke night for the neighborhood on Fridays, with free soft drinks and munchies. This might better be held at a neutral location, such as a community center or local bar.

- The church that offers excellent free one-day youth sports clinics with great food and amplified music (that local kids like) in partnership with the nearby Fellowship of Christian Athletes.

KIM: These are great examples, Paul! In our new-church experiences, we did several of these over the years. They are a lot of fun! New churches have to get their names and positive legends nailed down quickly, but it is also good for existing churches to continue this work! I'm glad you mentioned collaboration and cooperation as strategic ways of working within your community. Why should we reinvent the wheel when sometimes all we need to do is hitch our wagons together?

PAUL: It may be helpful for a church to focus on a theme in terms of the legend it seeks to create. That theme could be "community-engaged," "loves kids," "best music in town," "a happy place," or any number of other possibilities. When you are thinking up ministry and activity ideas, look for those that continue the storyline and add an element of surprise. Seek to build one strong legend in varied ways—don't jump all over the place. You may not have the people power to create more than one legend at a time and probably not more than two, unless you are a larger church.

I am not suggesting that highly motivated teams stop doing effective ministry simply because it does not advance the theme. But it is worth considering how that ministry carries the theme forward and, when possible, framing the ministry in terms of the theme.

KIM: One of the churches I coached is now using a bridge-building theme to promote its positive legend. In order to help them decide what things to do, they concluded that a ministry or idea has to fit into their theme. If it doesn't help to build a bridge somehow—from church to community, from church to unchurched, or from brokenness to wholeness—then they don't do it.

PAUL: Exactly. This need for positive legend is important for the church, but it is also important for the pastor who will lead this church in its next advance. The *new* pastor especially needs to create a legend! It is often wise for the pastor-parish or call committee to assist the new pastor in planning for this!

KIM: This is a great point—especially as it relates to that pastor support committee. So often these groups can really sabotage a pastor, rather than being the supportive group that can help a pastor succeed.

PAUL: Sometimes I find people on such committees who see sabotage as their role, although they call it "checks and balances." In fact, such committees exist not to police the pastor and ministry teams but rather to work with the pastor and ministry teams to imagine and to set up conditions for great and legendary ministry! We are all on the same side!

KIM: And cultivating the right lead team to oversee ministry can be a real challenge. In our tradition, the pastor is chair of the nominating process, so the balance of getting the right people on this team is tricky. Too many "yes" folks isn't good, and too many "no" people is just as bad. A well-balanced team of spiritually mature people who will both support and provide accountability is sometimes difficult to pull off!

PAUL: When pastors are getting started in a new place, they have a great opportunity to cultivate positive first impressions. The first perceptions may fall short of legendary but can still give the new pastor added credibility for the hard work of leading. In his book *A New Beginning for Pastors and Congregations*, Kennon L. Callahan tells about a mythical pastor who came to a new town and left his boxes packed for a few weeks, going straight to the hospital in his first hours in the community, discovering a family in crisis with a loved one in critical condition, and giving significant chaplain hours to the family.

Word went all over the place. The pastor unwittingly had created a sense of personal legend that would aid his ministry in that place, and would probably persist even as he shifted toward a ministry model that was less focused on chaplaincy in its approach (San Francisco: Jossey-Bass, 1999, chap. 1). Early perceptions are hard to bust.

KIM: One of the worst things that a new pastor can do is to say no to an opportunity for ministry—funerals, home visits, weddings, or hospital visits. Being available to meet people's needs is probably the best way to build positive perceptions and a good reputation. I talked with a pastor last week who attended Nora Lou's ninetieth birthday party on his first day in town; eighteen months later, folks are still talking about it!

PAUL: There are some really gifted pastors-in-formation, moving into their first place of service, who do not know this! Please take notice: getting the opportunity to lead a funeral for a community resident is like winning the lottery! Every pastor should do all that he or she can in the first six months in a new place to send the strong signal that people matter!

KIM: Definitely! It wasn't easy for Gary to do all those funerals that I mentioned in an earlier chapter. There were lots of interruptions to our life together that emergency situations bring, but it was the right thing to do in that ministry area.

PAUL: In my first six months at Gulf Breeze Church, getting to know what was already a 2,000-member church, I kept my office door open most of the time on the busy main corridor that ran through our church building. I ran that office like a Main Street shopkeeper, stopping my desk work to gab with anyone who walked by. This was not my preferred mode of operation, but I believed it would be valuable in the early months of relationship building. As the months wore on, I got very busy, networking more with prospective members than with current ones, and often off-site. I wanted to bring in 300 new members my third year there, and that would not happen with me keeping shop nine to five at the church. Soon I was busy developing our ministry infrastructure and eventually leading the charge to launch a new campus down the road. The office door eventually closed more, and then I moved my office to a remote musty building where I could get more work done, bequeathing my prime real estate to a new ministry that needed the space. But helpful perceptions were set and dozens of critical relationships strengthened in those early months on our church's Main Street.

KIM: There is just no way to build positive perceptions without being open and available to people. Today, social media can help us build an availableness without being physically present with people. Of course, you need to know when to put your phone or laptop away, too. Face-to-face meeting times are just too important to blow due to the distraction of a phone!

PAUL: Some pastors work Facebook like Andy Griffith glad-handing his way around the courthouse square, stopping to read postings on the Facebook pages of their parishioners and others and discovering numerous life issues and opportunities for pastoral care. They use Facebook to touch a lot of folks in a short time. And face-to-face coffee meetings often result.

One pastor I worked with had a great habit of getting on the phone for two hours every Sunday afternoon. Two hours. That was all. She would call worship visitors. She would call people whom she had missed that morning. She would call people who had a birthday coming up the following week. Short calls and long calls—you can easily make a dozen quality calls in two hours, plus at least that many voicemails. She grew a church from 100 to 400 in attendance in a decade with a whole series of good pastoral habits. But none was more integral to her church's growth than her two hours on the phone each Sunday. In my Gulf Breeze years, I did the same with worship visitors for a couple of hours on Monday nights. Week after week for years! The phone is a priceless tool for ministry.

KIM: Paul, I really don't like using the phone. I'm concerned about intruding and timing issues, but you make a valid point about using it as a ministry tool. I guess with answering machines and caller ID, you really don't need to feel that you are intruding on other people's lives.

PAUL: You have to know the appropriate boundaries in any context. Calling after 9:00 p.m. is too late in most cases, unless you are in a campus ministry setting, and you can move that back an hour or two. Often, people will not answer a strange caller ID, but you can still leave a warm message. And in all cases, we should use the pathways for contact that people have directly given to us. It is a good idea not to call, send e-mail, or Facebook people when someone else gives us that person's contact. As for mass mail, it's pretty harmless (and, many feel, pretty useless).

It may seem that we are picking a bit on pastors here, but we started this chapter's conversation by underlining the fact that both churches and pastors have reputations. So we should also stress those habits of life among key laity in a congregation that are just as significant in creating legend as what the pastor does!

I used to walk out of my office on Wednesday evenings through an adjacent room full of busy workers—all laity, and many not even church members—wrapping up donated books in brown paper to send to incarcerated people. They call it "Books for Prisoners." They work a couple of hours each week—but wow—what a great difference they make in the lives of a community behind bars. They have sent thousands of books into prisons. They work within our church's larger theme of justice and love toward our neighbors, especially those who are marginalized in society. A powerful witness! This kind of thing can give a church its street cred.

KIM: One of the themes emerging here is that creating legend does not necessarily take enormous time. What it really does take is an attitude that communicates, "It's really not about me."

Too many parking lot meetings and impromptu conversations at the grocery store end up being pastor-bashing or church-staff-bashing or just general church-bashing meetings. Most of these conversations have at their core, "It's really about me—what I want and how I think it should be done." The unfortunate part of these kinds of gatherings is that others really do hear what's being said. Just like those folks who went to the café to hear what was happening at your church, Paul! A church's reputation is also built by what the church people say about it!

This was mentioned earlier, and I think it bears repeating—a congregation's leadership team must speak positively about what is happening during a change season. The influence that leaders have within a congregation is huge, and they must take this seriously. Flippant comments can easily lead to gossip and rumormongering. I've worked in more than one church where the gossip mill ran like wildfire. In one situation, even the local bank employees were calling the church to find out what was happening, because of things church members were saying when they deposited their paychecks!

PAUL: We all have those moments when we disagree with this or that decision in our local church or with our denomination. But negative talk out in the community about our church, its staff, or our spiritual brothers and sisters is just *poisonous*. It is an assault on the body of Christ. I think we call it for what it is; it is just wrong. The biblical models are clear: we deal with our disagreements by talking to one another respectfully and discreetly; and even when we need a third party, we must respect that this is God's church we are talking about. Giving any church a public black eye is just a horrible idea. Even when we are part of somewhat public struggles for change in our church—as my congregation is with respect to policies in our denomination—I think we always need to speak lovingly, even affectionately, of our church and of those with whom we disagree. This feels very clear to me, Kim.

KIM: For me it boils down to one prayer: "Lord, what do you want to do through me for the growth of your kingdom on earth?" If we prayed this prayer and really listened and acted on God's responses, then we wouldn't have to have this conversation! Really!

PAUL: As we close out this section, two questions I want our readers to ask are these: "What is your church known for in your community?" and "What do you want your church to be known for?"

KIM: I would add a third: "What is my part in my church's reputation?"

PAUL: God strategically placed Jesus and countless others—whose lives inspire us by the way they made the right and sometimes surprising moves in their time and place—to get the world talking and paying close attention. They give us a rich playbook; there is very little we have to invent from scratch! And yet God calls us to follow tenaciously in their steps or in their spirit! And get the world talking!

"Since we are surrounded by so great a cloud of witnesses, . . . let us run with perseverance the race that is set before us" (Heb. 12:1 NRSV).

They went to Capernaum, and when the Sabbath came, Jesus went into the synagogue and began to teach. The people were amazed at his teaching, because he taught them as one who had authority, not as the teachers of the law. Just then a man in their synagogue who was possessed by an impure spirit cried out, "What do you want with us, Jesus of Nazareth? Have you come to destroy us? I know who you are—the Holy One of God!"

"Be quiet!" said Jesus sternly. "Come out of him!" The impure spirit shook the man violently and came out of him with a shriek.

The people were all so amazed that they asked each other, "What is this? A new teaching—and with authority! He even gives orders to impure spirits and they obey him." News about him spread quickly over the whole region of Galilee. (Mark 1:21-28 NIV)

Jesus commanded them not to tell anyone. But the more he did so, the more they kept talking about it. People were overwhelmed with amazement. "He has done everything well," they said. "He even makes the deaf hear and the mute speak." (Mark 7:36-37 NIV)

When they brought the colt to Jesus and threw their cloaks over it, he sat on it. Many people spread their cloaks on the road, while others spread branches they had cut in the fields. Those who went ahead and those who followed shouted,

"Hosanna!"

"Blessed is he who comes in the name of the Lord!"

"Blessed is the coming kingdom of our father David!"

"Hosanna in the highest!" (Mark 11:7-10 NIV)

Eight

HOLD DIFFICULT PEOPLE ACCOUNTABLE

A note appeared on Pastor Ed's desk the day before the church council meeting about adding a second worship service. It was an anonymous threat to say that if Ed continued on "his crusade to divide the church," several prominent members were prepared to withhold their tithes and offerings. Ed figured out who had placed the letter there: it was Randy, the church's largest donor. Ed paid Randy a visit at his small appliance store downtown. Ed was very calm and said to him, "Randy, I don't know that you wrote this, but I believe that you put this on my desk." Randy admitted that he had done so and went into a rant about how First Church had always had one service so that all the members could know one another. Ed responded that he understood this, but that sometimes churches try different strategies so that more people can know Christ, even if they don't all know one another intimately. Ed did not remain long, but he said, "Randy, you are a valuable part of our church, you and each person that you reference in your threat. But this is properly a matter for the church council to discuss and decide without anonymous letters and threats."

The next night at the meeting, during the discussion of the matter, Ed surprised Randy by standing to read the anonymous letter. Ed never gave any indication that Randy was involved, but he read the letter in its entirety, including the threats to withhold donations. He then said, "Regardless of what decisions we *make, I hope we can recommit to one another to speak honestly, openly, and without resorting to threats." Ten minutes later the council voted 18 to 3 to begin the new service, and Randy left fuming, choosing to leave First Church after having spent all forty-seven years of his life there and to take his $30,000 annual pledge with him. In the following three months, no one else withdrew from giving or participation, but about four dozen new participants began attending the new service. Some of them began to contribute, and others stepped up as well. The church ended the year in the black. And they never looked back.*

KIM: Throughout the process of interviewing United Methodist congregations for our Toward Vitality research project, the most interesting part of the stories that people tell me has to do with how they handle difficult church members. Later in this chapter, we mention the difference between members and disciples, and this is most obvious when there is some conflict or challenge between people. Every group of leaders who has been interviewed has told me that in their process of renewal, revitalization, or revisioning, people left. In every one! It seems to be inevitable that in order to change the culture of a local congregation, someone is going to get upset or act badly or simply fade away. And the sad reality is that, in most instances, the leaving is a good thing.

PAUL: I guess it is a sad reality in one respect, but I also find this a very hopeful reality—that most churches are able to thrive and leap forward without the big bucks and the big attitude that a few members have used for years to control things. Hostage-taking behavior is always sad, but courage on the part of church leaders to refuse playing hostage to bullies, that makes me want to open the window and shout happy things!

But I have a question: how do good people become bullies in the first place? I don't think many people just wake up one morning and put on their Ray-Ban sunglasses and decide to be a bully. What's the motivation?

KIM: In an earlier chapter, we talked about fear as a motivation that often causes churches to stay stuck in the ruts in which they find themselves. I believe that fear is also the motivation behind some of the bad behavior that we experience. One person I interviewed spoke of the pervasive fear that she found among the older members of her congregation. She noted that as they become older and less able to get around, they sit at home and watch the news, which simply preys on their fears and magnifies those fears to levels from which they cannot recover! Many of these elders of the church still have enough influence and control to spread their fears throughout the congregation.

PAUL: I would agree that heavy doses of some forms of media work to instill a siege mentality in people, and they begin to see almost every new idea or new practice as part of an attack on the foundations of the world as they know it. When we look back at the folks who hounded Jesus, we should remember that they were part of a nation under military and political occupation by a very cruel empire. They didn't have to listen to talk radio 24/7 to feel under siege. They *were* under siege! A part of the way that they coped with the stress of life as an occupied people was to rally around certain religious and cultural traditions, often placing huge symbolic value in arcane rules and outward behaviors and losing touch at times with the spirit and purpose of their own religion. Jesus called them on this.

KIM: Also, for every bully that you find in a church, you often find twenty others who are afraid of hurting people's feelings, of losing people from their circles of friends, of having those who fund ministries withhold their money.

PAUL: The fear of rocking the boat really gives the bully power to rock the boat, while the rest of the group works to look past him or her and pretend that the boat is not rocking.

And God forbid that we should hurt the bully's feelings! That might upset someone else, and then the whole network of church relationships unravels. This kind of thinking explains how churches get stuck and find themselves unwilling to do rather obvious things that would help them thrive in ministry.

So we have named two fears so far that feed bullying behavior: fear of change in general and fear of upsetting anyone. What other fears do you see?

KIM: I see both fear of failure and fear of success!

PAUL: I can see fear of failure. But fear of success? Say more.

KIM: Success is an interesting beast. I think of the Israelites right after they walked across the sea to start their new life on the way to the Promised Land. They experienced the success of the adventure at this point; they had escaped and Pharaoh's army was wiped out. The fear of success came when they realized that they could not go back, and that fear caused them to wander around the wilderness for forty years. While they were successful at the start, their fear made them lose trust in God's promises, and they floundered through a whole generation of people.

A great illustration of this success fear came very early in my married life, while my husband and I were serving a small rural church during our seminary experience. The congregation came together in very positive ways to host a spaghetti supper that was to support a family in the community with financial needs due to a medical issue. The supper was a success in every way—the congregation's support for organizing, cooking, hosting, everything! The funds that were raised were substantial. The goodwill in the community was apparent.

So, at the next leader's meeting an idea was expressed that we do this kind of thing for another need in the community (which, here, meant outside the congregation). The conversation was lively and encouraging about this ministry. Then one woman spoke up. She asked, "If we keep doing this for people, when will it ever end?" Within minutes, the conversation turned and any hope of doing this kind of ministry was over. I still hurt about this because it changed the hopeful attitude of that congregation and its community.

PAUL: I would have been tempted to say back to her, "This will end when we get tired, but I am not tired yet. If some of you want to take a break for the next dinner, that's fine. But I bet some of us would like to keep doing all the good we can!" If just one person had said anything like that...I am guessing that the dinners would not have stopped. But I am also guessing that the woman who spoke up was a bit intimidating and that people were scared to cross her.

KIM: And as the pastor and spouse—we were in our early twenties! Simply not grown enough to talk back!

We live in a world that is surrounded by and bombarded with supposed fears. Some of these fears are not real. How did anyone know what would happen if that congregation continued to host dinners to help people? How do we know for sure that people will not like us or not give their money or any of the other things we are afraid of? They are made-up circumstances in our minds that paralyze us and keep us from being the bold disciples that we were created to be.

So what responses work against fear? There are many successful examples of gentle, kind, and helpful ways that people's fears can be addressed and bold moves can be made.

One such response is good communication. When church leaders move a congregation through change, it cannot be done in a vacuum. People must know what is going on and why it is happening. Many congregations invite all members and attendees to open meetings to discuss changes and give opportunity to ask questions and address fears. Regular information needs to be shared in as many ways as possible—e-mail, texts, Facebook pages, phone calls, newsletters—however your church communicates and as often as your church communicates. Even when you as a church leader think everyone should know about the change and you can stop talking about it, you need to keep doing it!

PAUL: I don't think you can overly communicate, especially in congregations of less than 200 worshipers. When big decisions get made finally, if they are made without everyone knowing what's going on, people feel as if something sneaky happened. And it just goes downhill from there.

KIM: A group of leaders at First UMC in College Station, Texas, told me that when they experienced a new vision and purpose for their congregation, several members began to cast doubts and stand against the proposed change. These leaders told me how they gently talked with those who were scared to encourage them that God was leading and there was no need for fear. They also held up the positive experiences and testimonies of changed lives as a result of their new vision in order to let the congregation know how God was leading and moving throughout the work.

So, when you experience some grumbling and discord among your congregation, work to find the root of that grumbling. You may find that some sense of fear has taken over, and I think I remember Jesus having some very clear words about fear—Don't go there! I am with you!

PAUL: Nearly two decades ago, when you could still count multisite congregations on your fingers, my church voted to build a second campus eight miles from the first and to do ministry in two locations. We let people wrestle with it before the vote. There was a 90 percent vote in the church's administrative body. Then we decided to take it to the whole church for further confirmation, since it was a big, expensive deal. So we had more conversation, more discernment, and the whole church voted 90 percent in favor of the proposal. The 10 percent were left frustrated and grumbling. They were afraid of all kinds of things, but we in the leadership never demonized them. We sat (for hours) and listened to them. We treated them respectfully. We agreed to disagree with them, but still to care for them—and there were some really super human beings among that 10 percent. The vote was over, and yet we still spent time with some of these folks, listening to them vent. We didn't need their votes, but we cared for them. Our pastoral charge was to help them process their fears, at least those who wanted to talk. It would have been more than appropriate for a few of them to leave, but not one of them chose to do so. And in time, they made peace with the changes, and we all moved on.

KIM: That's a great example, Paul! I've heard from other pastors that continuing to offer an ear and plain old pastoral care goes a long way to helping churches move through change obstacles.

Another obstacle to change within a congregation has to do with the difference between church members and disciples. George Barna's research has been telling us for years that there is little difference in the behaviors of secular people and churchgoers. Greed, pride, envy, gossip, and all sorts of nastiness have invaded our congregations. This invasion happened because we were not holding people accountable to Christian discipleship and behavior. We've been busy being nice to one another and have allowed a host of bad behaviors that have no place in Christian communities.

PAUL: Which leads me to wonder how nice it is for us to tolerate really bad behavior. But continue!

KIM: As a ministry coach, I have been practicing asking good questions as a way to help my clients come to their own answers. This is a useful tool in the arena of bad behavior, too, and I often encourage pastors to practice asking these questions: How does that attitude reflect your Christian discipleship? What does that statement tell us about how you understand Scripture? How do you think a follower of Jesus would respond to that issue? When you ask one of these questions, allow the silence that follows. Don't answer the question for the other person. Let him or her wrestle with the fact that you want an answer! If needed, give her or him a few days' grace to come up with an answer.

PAUL: Kim, a lot of members in our churches do not think of themselves as Jesus followers. And this has happened precisely because we have gone far too many years—decades, in some churches—without asking the kinds of questions you just raised!

KIM: At a training event where tables of church leaders were wrestling with some of the obstacles they were facing toward change, one group wanted to know how they should respond to the people in their congregation who were concerned about "those" people who might come into their church as a result of the proposed outreach vision. I suggested that they ask these people what they think heaven will look like. Who do they think they will find there?

PAUL: If people only knew the whole story about the nice-looking folks who are sitting just down the church pew from them, singing along with them on Sunday morning! My Lord! I have sometimes looked across the room to a particular row, knowing something about the respective politics, criminal histories, or the love lives of the various people on a particular row and chuckled at the possible train wreck that would occur if they knew the rest of the story on each other! This is one fragile enterprise—the church of Jesus Christ!

KIM: Granted, we are all on a journey, and none of us is ever going to complete that journey to be a fully perfect Christian disciple. But if we ignore the obviously un-Christian behavior of our fellow church members, how do we ever expect to make any progress, let alone bring anyone else with us?

Power, or perceived power, is another obstacle to change within congregations. Lately I have been wrestling with the difference between people who operate from a sense of power and those who work from a leadership mindset. My sense is that power people operate mainly out of ego and agenda. Leaders tend to operate from a sense of vision and purpose for a greater good.

So what do you do when you run up against power people? Truthfully, these are the ones who typically leave when they don't get their own way, and the best thing to do is let them.

PAUL: It is clear that Jesus was unwilling to be held hostage or to allow his movement to be held hostage by obstinate people. He let them walk. When they behaved badly or said ridiculous things, he was not afraid to finish the conversation in public, holding them publicly accountable for bad behavior or absurd theology. Jesus played hardball at this point. I assume that this played into the anger (within the religious establishment) and that it even may have fueled collusion with the Romans to execute Jesus.

But in the short run, this strategy helped Jesus' movement to gain momentum. It made the issues clearer, and it diminished the power of people whose vision was contrary to the movement.

KIM: Often in a coaching conversation, the opportunity arises to remind a pastor that he or she is the spiritual leader of the congregation. Being the spiritual leader allows opportunities to ask good, deep questions; to probe at the "niceness" that keeps us stuck; and to help us look to God for the answers to our questions. A few well-placed lay leaders who are comfortable in their own deep relationship with God can be spiritual leaders, too!

PAUL: So what can a church do to resist allowing people to subvert God's movement?

KIM: I can think of four right off the bat: (1) Set tenure limits on leadership positions, so that power positions are changed every three or four years. (2) Create clear job descriptions for church staff with regular supervision and accountability. (3) Mobilize leaders around the vision, so that more key people gravitate toward the center of church life and to key positions. (4) And pray. Pray for the church to bend its heart and its will to the mind of Christ. Prayer will intimidate people with a less-than-Christ-centered agenda.

PAUL: And to all that, I say, "Amen." Especially praying through until consensus is found. Back to the woman who didn't want to do any community dinners: a little praying would have marginalized her whining, and the church would have moved forward.

And above all, when people act out, gently but firmly hold them accountable for what they say and do! Little is served in ignoring it.

> Later Jesus and his disciples were at home having supper with a collection of disreputable guests. Unlikely as it seems, more than a few of them had become followers. The religion scholars and Pharisees saw him keeping this kind of company and lit into his disciples: "What kind of example is this, acting cozy with the riff-raff?"
>
> Jesus, overhearing, shot back, "Who needs a doctor: the healthy or the sick? I'm here inviting the sin-sick, not the spiritually-fit."

> The disciples of John and the disciples of the Pharisees made a practice of fasting. Some people confronted Jesus: "Why do the followers of John and the Pharisees take on the discipline of fasting, but your followers don't?"
>
> Jesus said, "When you're celebrating a wedding, you don't skimp on the cake and wine. You feast. Later you may need to pull in your belt, but not now. As long as the bride and groom are with you, you have a good time. No one throws cold water on a friendly bonfire. This is Kingdom Come!" (Mark 2:15-20 *THE MESSAGE*)

Nine

SHOW UP AT THE PARTIES

Doris graduated seminary on her sixtieth birthday, feeling about thirty-five years old and ready to change the world. She had accepted her first call to a church of sixty members, with thirty-five in attendance. A sign surely! They could not quite meet minimum salary guidelines, but Doris had a little savings from her earlier career. At any rate, she had not taken the turn into parish ministry "for the money." When she arrived in Cherry Blossom, Illinois, about sixty miles from the western edge of the Chicago bright lights, she discovered a quiet parish that rarely mixed with people outside their own quiet circles. Doris fell in love with them easily.

Ever the party girl, Doris began to look for friends in Cherry Blossom who knew how to have a little fun. Within three months, she had managed her way into the social scene—her gift to Cherry Blossom was a wonderful sense of humor and a genuine appreciation of decidedly irreverent people. The rumors of the people she was befriending began to puzzle her congregation, but she seemed perfectly normal (a.k.a. boring) on Sundays, so they let it go for a while. In the fall, however, a few of the more colorful folks began showing up for worship. This alarmed some in the parish, but they pretended to be "happy to see them in church."

Meanwhile, in addition to hitting the parties, Doris began to show up for causes that she believed in and to bring volunteers to work—mostly from the parties, not so much from the church. Within six months, she was deeply involved in the local food movement's lobbying campaign with the downtown grocery store and with the city park renovation project. The town took Doris seriously because she always recruited volunteers for the things she believed in. By the time a few of the more prudish folks at the church decided to confront Doris for paying more attention to the townsfolk than to the parishioners, it was too late. By then, many of the townsfolk were involved at Cherry Blossom Church, and a new day had arrived. Doris had staged a coup before most of her staid little flock figured out what was coming—and with an army of friends from the bars, the country club, and the varied local community action groups. Within six years, Cherry Blossom Church had tripled in size, and only about fifteen of the original cast remained. No longer did the church sit on the community sidelines like wallflowers. They were now in the thick of community life and were renewed as a church for another generation.

PAUL: Doris's story was vintage Jesus. Jesus showed up not only in the places of weeping but also in the happy places.

KIM: Way to go, Doris! I'm wondering, though, what might have happened had Doris been a bit more intentional about bringing her church people along for the ride? One of the strategies for church development is how you "velcro" people together—people from different social groups, who interact in new ways for new purposes. It sounds as if Doris was doing what came naturally to her. Yet I wonder if interacting with people in different venues could be more intentional—or maybe that just takes the fun out of it!

PAUL: I would bet that Doris had at least one church member who could have been a sidekick for most of her forays into community. In creating a culture of mentoring and apprenticing, we should always keep our eyes open for the *bright eyes* who are ready to come alongside us.

A few weeks ago, I was sitting in the Edgewater neighborhood of Chicago at a Mexican café with Rich Gorman, a church planter with Community Christian Church. Rich is breaking many of the rules as he plants an Edgewater campus for Community Christian. The church is known for an attractional model of church planting, in which you go in big and gather a worship crowd quickly. Rich is pioneering a new way of planting for them, in order to reach a different slice of the population. As he builds relationships with community folks, he has discovered that there is enormous value in showing up in the places where the community celebrates and has positive passion. So he hangs out at bars and shows up to work with environmental groups. And he brings people from the bar to the environmental action meeting. This gains him credibility with people where pastors generally have little credibility. And from this, he is building a church.

KIM: See, Rich is doing this intentionally! I know that church planters often have to do this work—at the beginning stages, it is all they do!

PAUL: For a church to be planted, it has to get rooted in community.

KIM: So how can we do this work of partying and building relationships in existing congregations?

PAUL: Well, to begin with, I think we need to recognize the same urgency for this task in and around the established church as would exist in and around a new-church initiative. Without vital community roots, no church can thrive.

I recall the first church I served as a full-time pastor. On my first day in town, even as the moving truck was still in front of the house, I left home to visit a church member at the hospital before his surgery—a patriarch with quite a few children in the church and community. From that visit to Papa on my first day in town, goodwill was planted with that family that lasted my entire time there. However, a few weeks later, a week after our son was born, I was on paternity leave, and a member of our church had her ninetieth birthday. I chose to skip the party. Everyone understood—it did not become an issue—but in my heart I knew then, and I learned across the years in other experiences, that when you miss a ninety-year-old woman's birthday party, you are missing as much of an opportunity as when you miss her funeral a few years later! What I know about Jesus is that he would have surely made the party—and he may or may not have altered his plans to hit the funeral.

KIM: Yes! From the very beginning it is so important for pastors to begin building relationships. I've heard many people share stories about how their new pastors came to events just to be there to listen and learn. Paul Escamilla at St. John's United Methodist Church in Austin, Texas, is still being praised by his congregation because he did go to a ninetieth birthday party when the moving van was in the driveway! The goodwill he established with this new congregation on the very first day gave him an opportunity to move them in creative ways to even more outward-focused ministries.

PAUL: You make friends at parties. It's just that simple. Some of those friends become allies. A few invariably become church members. In other cases, you become someone they may choose to trust or turn to when they hit a crisis in their life the next week or the next year.

I celebrated my birthday in Yosemite National Park a few years back. I was part of a group of friends, mostly strangers to me at the start of the week. The group was related to a running club; people brought their kids, and we created a little community in the Curry Village campground for a few days. We hiked; we rafted; we sat around the campfire in the evenings. As the week progressed, the rumor passed from one to another that I was a minister. Now this was a decidedly nonreligious group of people, and so they were a bit fascinated by me—that I was just like them in so many ways. They fascinated me, too. It was mutual.

On the hiking trails, one after another, they would come up and begin to walk alongside me and talk about their lives. By the campfire, they would pull up a lawn chair and talk about spirituality, especially after a couple drinks loosened their tongues.

I had more meaningful pastoral conversations in that week than I might discover in several years of pastoral ministry, sequestered among the church folks. It was one of the great discovery weeks of my life.

KIM: Gary and I have had similar experiences during vacations, even on dates—when the needs of a server become a great opportunity to listen and offer prayer support! Gary is great at conversation with strangers; his best stories tell of how God opens a holy opportunity while Gary is flying across the country!

PAUL: Gary always is telling a story about his airplane friends; then the other day, I had a Gary Shockley–style encounter with the flight attendant on a cross-country flight. It was a little like Jesus' great conversation with the woman at the well in John 4. It was just a great series of short conversations, ending in the woman accepting my invitation to attend a church that I work with in her neighborhood back home. Had it not been for all the parties I attended over the last few years, I am not sure that my conversation with the flight attendant would have played out the way it did. You see, I did not grow up going to parties.

KIM: Me neither, only extended family gatherings.

PAUL: My mother is an introvert. We had close friends over at the house, but we didn't do big parties. In fact, my mother tells me that I opted each year not to have a birthday party after age eight. In retrospect, perhaps ours was not a party house, and birthday parties did not seem to fit there. My mother is a jewel, but Doris would not have taken Mom along to any of her parties.

I am now fifty years old, and one of the key components of my life and my ministry in the second quarter century is that I throw and attend parties. It really shifted after that week at Yosemite. Now, every few months I fill up my condo or the roof deck of our building with people—some of whom I don't even know. I live in Chinatown in DC, and our Chinese New Year party is now a staple of life for the fifty or sixty other people who attend. I also find myself constantly attending dinner parties, birthday parties, going-away parties, PhD graduation parties, various seasonal parties—sometimes two or three in a weekend.

Granted, I live in a town of decidedly interesting people and some of the best stories on the planet. One of our friends works at the White House. Another works with world-famous recording artists in New York City. A very good friend, no longer in town, was a major writer of the Affordable Care Act for the House of Representatives in 2009. Always interesting stories! Occasionally you meet someone who reports directly to someone famous, and you get a tidbit that *The Washington Post* has not yet reported. But the point of the party is to share joy and to build community with people beyond rigid social boundaries. I have rarely held a party in recent years without there being Christians, Muslims, Buddhists, Taoists, and (in DC) plenty of atheists. I would have it no other way.

KIM: We did the same thing during our Nashville years. There were several neighbors around us who had a variety of backgrounds and lifestyles. It is a great evening to have several people over for dinner and conversation. Sometimes we get the board games out and play something that is fun for everyone! As a pastor's wife, it has been quite refreshing to get "outside the box" of gathering just with church people! I'm learning about and loving people at a much different level than when I stay within my safe group of church friends. Who knows what God may do with these relationships? I can say that all of these people feel free to stop by our porch for a casual chat from time to time.

PAUL: I sometimes joke that my fourth church plant is this community of people that I might name "The Church of the Chinese New Year Party." Often toward the end of a party, I find myself in conversation in the corner of the room with someone who is dealing with some sort of personal crisis (often related to family relationships) or who wants to talk about God. In the twenty-first century, it is easy and natural to talk about anything at a DC party. It's not socially acceptable to get pushy about religion. To do so would be perceived as creepy. You allow space for people to be themselves, to express themselves, and because the point is not to convert anyone, the depth of the relationships and the influence grow all the stronger.

KIM: Definitely! I find that when I listen and ask good questions, I am often allowing God to speak in the conversation. It really isn't about me, but about how God uses me in the midst of relationships.

PAUL: And honestly, in all great relationships, each person is changed by the encounter—each person brings something to the table that transforms the other. I think that is also what keeps me throwing and attending parties with eclectic people. Not only does God use me as a positive building block in other people's lives, but also these eclectic people give me new insights, new energy, new wisdom, and new joy. The gifts are mutual! "The Church of the Chinese New Year Party." You and Gary should come sometime.

KIM: Can't wait!

PAUL: The point of all this is that there is power in building a constituency of goodwill and shared values and life experience beyond the congregation. It roots a leader in a community, even before it roots a church. In some cases, it gives that leader cover, so to speak, when a few of the controllers at the church begin to push back. I do believe that Jesus would have been gone in a year had it not been for the crowds of people who loved him beyond the walls of the religious institutions.

KIM: We experienced this very thing in our church in north central Pennsylvania. In this small mountain town there was very little for young adults (as we were then) to do on the weekends, except go to bars. As we built relationships with young people, our house became the place to hang out on Friday nights. We played cards and board games, we talked and laughed, and we shared our stories and our sorrows. We partied on a regular basis, always making room for new relationships that were developing.

Those relationships made most of the change in that congregation possible—because of the trust and friendships and energy for ministry that developed. I guess it would be no surprise to you, Paul, that several of these folks are now pastors serving their own congregations!

PAUL: No surprise at all!

Three days later there was a wedding in the village of Cana in Galilee. Jesus' mother was there. Jesus and his disciples were guests also. When they started running low on wine at the wedding banquet, Jesus' mother told him, "They're just about out of wine."

Jesus said, "Is that any of our business, Mother—yours or mine? This isn't my time. Don't push me."

She went ahead anyway, telling the servants, "Whatever he tells you, do it."

Six stoneware water pots were there, used by the Jews for ritual washings. Each held twenty to thirty gallons. Jesus ordered the servants, "Fill the pots with water." And they filled them to the brim.

"Now fill your pitchers and take them to the host," Jesus said, and they did.

When the host tasted the water that had become wine (he didn't know what had just happened but the servants, of course, knew), he called out to the bridegroom, "Everybody I know begins with their finest wines and after the guests have had their fill brings in the cheap stuff. But you've saved the best till now!"

This act in Cana of Galilee was the first sign Jesus gave, the first glimpse of his glory. (John 2:1-11 *THE MESSAGE*)

PAUL: And I would add, this showed not only a first glimpse of his glory, but also his style. The guy knew how to enjoy a party!

Ten

TRUST GOD AND EXPECT GREAT THINGS

They said Pastor Brad walked into Trinity Church a bit like a Kansas gunslinger from the 1870s. To some, he just seemed wonderfully confident and full of hope for Trinity's future, like a new sheriff come to town. To others, he seemed cocky and a bit egocentric. Some asked, "Who does he think he is, as if this church is going to grow now that he's here?" But most folks found him to be an engaging preacher. On his fourth Sunday at Trinity, his sermon text was from Joel 2:25: "I will repay you for the years that the swarming locust has eaten" (NRSV). It was a great sermon by almost all counts. Even the skeptics wanted to believe that Brad's vision of a renewed and thriving Trinity Church was from God. Brad was a likeable guy, and he seemed convinced that God would bless Trinity's future. Almost everyone began rooting for Brad and for Trinity.

A year and a half later, Trinity's worship attendance had surged from 170 to almost 300 per week. Trinity was still nowhere near its historic peak of 1,200 per week fifty years earlier. But Brad had generated hopefulness, unseen in five decades, simply by believing in great things. In no respect did he lead the church to expect the 1950s to return—in fact, he convened a vision team to take a hard look at the new community that lived around the church facility and to think about radically innovative approaches to ministry. The sheer force of Brad's faith in the possible caused others to believe as well. And soon, believing was seeing.

KIM: When I was growing up, my mom created a culture of routine. Each day of the week had its own tasks and responsibilities. We all knew which days the sheets were washed, when the house would be clean, and when new food would appear in the pantry. I could have easily become that kind of person, and I would have been quite happy living in routine. But I married a man who is a change agent! So after several years of struggling to maintain routines, I finally gave up and began to be more comfortable with the diversity and chaos that comes in living with change.

PAUL: I grew up with a father much like your husband. In fact, my dad, your husband, and Pastor Brad have a lot in common.

When I was eight, Dad announced that our family was moving west to Southern California, where he had accepted a position as pastor of a growing congregation. In August of 1970, on that first wild and wonderful car journey westward, watching the landscape transform from Texas prairie to desert mountains and then to orange groves, I caught Dad's spirit of adventure.

In our family we trust God, we take prayerful risks, and we expect good things. Our family's risk in moving to California turned out wonderfully. We each thrived as human beings, and Magnolia Avenue Church quadrupled in its size and community impact!

Of all the risky endeavors that I have tried since then, some worked out better than others. But I have become ever more convinced across the years that when we seek to live on the cutting edge of God's will, God blesses us and blesses the tasks that we put our hands to. *I also have come to believe that God will prosper the ministry of any church that is willing to go with God wherever its faithfulness requires.*

I am aware that many folks are not wired to take risks—even many of the bright-eyed people are not wired this way. I think a lot of it has to do with past experience, especially how we were raised.

KIM: So true. In local congregations, a lot of great folks are wired to get comfortable or to get the church into a comfortable resting place as soon as possible. And then just about the time they get comfortable with where the church is heading, something changes and they are tossed up in the air again, not knowing how they will get to the next comfortable spot where they can kick back and fall into routine. Sometimes that comfortable routine is an understanding that "church" is what we do on Sunday mornings, period. We lose sight of the surprise factor of being Jesus in our world today.

PAUL: You have reminded me of a new church planted near Houston a few years back. According to their pastor, setting up for worship each week in their first few years, "they moved enough chairs to fill the Astrodome twice." And then one day they moved into a building with permanent chairs. They were able to stop hauling chairs, to sit down, and to catch their breath. And from that day, they also stopped growing. And they made themselves quite comfortable.

KIM: For several years I led congregations through a renewal process called *ReFocusing*, produced by Church Resource Ministries. One part of that process is a basic understanding of what happens in a situation when we bump up against change. Most often, when anyone faces change, it is first felt as a threat to our security: "I'm happy in my routine, and this change will affect how I live in my routine." Usually we react to these threats to our security with emotional and sometimes irrational responses, until someone comes along and suggests that we look for information about the issue.

So we study and learn and analyze and come to a place where we feel we have some understanding of what it is that we are truly facing. Once we have an understanding, then we can look for information again—this time it will be information that will help us solve our problem. When we have information and understanding together, then we can feel secure as we begin to develop a plan that will lead us to a place where we can be comfortable.

Often the plan involves some new program that was developed in another church. We start the new program and sit back as leaders of the congregation say, "Whew! Glad that is over! We are back in control again because we have this great new program that will help us be a wonderful church!" What we really have done is maintain a sense of control that serves only to further feed our need to feel secure. We are spinning on a merry-go-round that starts with a breach of security and proceeds with new learning and studying, whirling around to new plans and programs that lead us back to a secure place again—where we are in control.

PAUL: This sounds quite familiar. There are a zillion seminars out there to educate us on postmodern whatever and train us in the next program that will save our church's rear end.

But it *is* a merry-go-round: it never seems to stop at the point where we feel secure—it keeps going!

KIM: Exactly. Here's an example: Anytown Church somewhere in Arizona is experiencing the summer budget pinch. They know that this happens every year because the snowbirds have gone back to Michigan and many regulars are on vacation. So the leaders look around and wonder how they will be able to make it to the end of the year! They quickly decide that the best solution would be a fund-raiser of some sort, but it has to happen when people are starting to come back to the area. The pastor tells a story of his previous church back east where they raised lots of money by selling pumpkins during the month of October, using the church lawn as a pumpkin patch. The team gathers the information necessary to get pumpkins, design a patch, and recruit volunteers to sell pumpkins. October arrives, and soon after a big pumpkin truck rolls into town. The church sells pumpkins and has a wonderful success for their church budget. All is well—we are back in control again!

But, Paul, there is one big problem with this way of approaching church security breaches—it never ends! It is a dizzying process of racing around in a circle from security breach to understanding to control and onto the next threat or crisis. Most of the church leadership teams in this country are dizzy because they have been around this circle so many times.

PAUL: Merry-go-rounds can be dizzying, and they don't really take us anywhere! Many church leadership teams are not just dizzy but also exhausted because they are running the same programs with dwindling volunteers and diminishing returns on all the effort.

KIM: Most churches are finding that they simply cannot do enough fast enough to manage the security threats that keep coming, faster and faster than ever before in the twenty-first century. But there is another way!

PAUL: Thank God.

KIM: In some ways this other way is harder. In some ways this other way is much easier. It is harder because we have to admit that we are not in control—we have never been in control—and we have to give up the idea of being in control. We have to surrender God's church back to God. As individuals and as a corporate leadership team we all have to realize that our local congregation is and always has been God's, and we have to give it back to God! This is the way that God intends the church to be. Romans 12:1 encourages us to be living sacrifices. Proverbs 3:5 says, "Trust in the LORD with all your heart; don't rely on your own intelligence" (CEB).

PAUL: This sounds like the first of the Twelve Steps. Most of us will not go to the place of letting go and trusting God until *life as it is* has become entirely unmanageable and unacceptable to us. I see more and more churches coming to this place, to a place where something has to give. We are at a crisis moment where a significant percentage of American churches will cease to exist within a decade or two unless something gives. Some of those churches will go out of business before the key leaders stop to acknowledge that they are not in control.

KIM: When we are willing to surrender our congregations back to God, amazing things happen. But this is not the way of the quick fix to restore a sense of security. This is about stepping off the security merry-go-round. It is about waiting and watching and listening for what God has to say to us. It is a good idea for multiple leaders to keep a prayer journal during this time—capturing thoughts and leanings and things that they see or hear that may be a direction from God. Each person needs to be keenly attuned to finding God in the midst of each day. It is always amazing to me, when folks get together to share their prayer journals, how God has a similar message that is shared corporately. When a church works through a season of prayerful discernment, I have never yet seen such a church spin off in a multitude of directions. When we pray and listen and watch, God honors our dedication with God's revelation and a sense of common direction and focus.

PAUL: I saw this lived out in my own congregation a couple of years ago, truly an amazing thing. We were faced with a decision that could easily have divided us into two factions. But we prayed for six months and shared what we were hearing. Then when the time came to decide the way forward, there was almost total consensus. And a sense of peace pervaded our church, despite our knowledge that we were taking enormous risks. We knew that no matter what happened, God had led us to this point and nothing would happen that God was unable to handle. Church doesn't get better than this.

KIM: Thanks, Paul, that is exactly what I am talking about—it's a different kind of security.

> What, then, shall we say in response to these things? If God is for us, who can be against us? He who did not spare his own Son, but gave him up for us all—how will he not also, along with him, graciously give us all things? (Rom 8:31-32 NIV)

The most valuable thing that a congregation has to offer is an ongoing relationship with God through Jesus Christ. The mission of the church is to make disciples of Jesus Christ for the transformation of the world. So our security can finally be only in Christ, whose promise is always to be with us. This is the easy part of surrender.

PAUL: What's the hard part?

KIM: We have to take action. It's so much more than "Kum Ba Yah." We surrender. We listen. We discover new revelation. We are able to see ourselves and to see our community in new ways. We find direction. Then we have to follow. We have to go there. We have to take action and sometimes that action is letting go. I can't say this strongly enough—sometimes we have to let go of programs and activities that we have been doing for a long time that just aren't bringing it anymore. It is fear that keeps us from letting go, and fear is the opposite of trust. So we can't trust God if we won't let go!

PAUL: You referred to this as alignment in chapter 1, the spiritual posture after surrender in Gary Mays's "Four Postures of Spiritual Authority," putting new discoveries into action. It sometimes takes some courage. It's often easier just to go back inside and sing another stanza.

KIM: And sometimes it is easier just to adopt someone else's program. If my church picks up the program that your church has done successfully, then we miss the opportunity to discover what it is that God strategically has for us to do in our community. We shortchange our own ability to be strategic with God by not doing the hard work of discovery!

The book of Joshua is a great study in courage. Six times God tells Joshua to be strong and have courage—"for I am always with you." That is a promise that we can carry with us today!

PAUL: Interesting. Joshua was taking people into really strange territory. Into scary territory! I think about my dad, again, the guy who taught me to take risks with God. Many of the leaders who I coach today are up to things that would disorient my father and, in a few cases, terrify him. His sense of ministry frontier forty years ago is settled land today. God is leading churches in our time to some places far beyond that frontier of the 1970s. Far beyond! The world has changed so much in the last four decades!

KIM: Yes, the change is dizzying!

PAUL: It is really easy to find ourselves motivated by fear in times of such dramatic change, even when that has never really been our style in the past—to run on fear.

KIM: And it is easy to find ourselves looking to the past, even when we have considered ourselves progressive and forward-looking people! One of the churches that I coached in Florida experienced this process of surrender. It was a small congregation, inward in its thinking. The people had forgotten what their community looked like. They were so used to it that they had ceased seeing it. When they surrendered, God helped them see the real needs within their community with fresh eyes. This revelation led them to do two things:

- First, they planned a weekly Wednesday night dinner and study time focused on encouraging and equipping adult attendees to step up their ability to be the hands and feet of Jesus in their daily lives. Age-appropriate activities were offered for youth and children, with a similar focus: making a difference in the neighborhood. (Kids ate free, in order to encourage family participation.)

- Second, they partnered with the local elementary school to be active volunteers wherever the school needed help.

Today that church has a vibrant ministry outside the walls of the church building. And the community sees the church as a positive place. This is a huge change!

Another congregation, through surrender, saw a need to be more active in ministry with and for poor people in their county, many of whom had lost jobs and homes in the recession. By building partnerships with county agencies and other churches, the church began to use the fellowship hall as a cold-night shelter for the homeless population in their community. They actually provided temporary living space for a few people. They began to build relationships with those they served and actively to help people get back on their feet.

PAUL: I am working with folks who are even surrendering and giving up the practice of large-venue public worship, discovering new ways to practice

Word and Sacrament: smaller ways, simpler ways, multiplying ways, ways that enable them to make disciples in a new land and to serve the people in their mission zone.

Kim, what do you see to be the difference between these kinds of constructive and somewhat adventurous initiatives you describe and the security-blanket programs that churches cling to on the merry-go-round?

KIM: The difference is that some initiatives are empowered by the Holy Spirit within the lives of folks who are willing to partner with God to make a difference in their communities. The work of these congregations is intentional toward making disciples and being the hands and feet of Jesus for people whom they don't even know yet. *These churches are doing such ministry not in order to save their church but in order to serve God and their neighbors.* That is a critical point. This is where loving one another, loving your community, and living out your calling come together!

PAUL: So it's a community orientation instead of a saving-the-church-as-we-know-it orientation.

KIM: Yes! These congregations have given up saving their church.

PAUL: Wow. That's the critical shift. I think about when Jesus told us that when we dare to lose our lives for his sake, we find life.

KIM: These churches have chosen to trust God and in many ways to give away their ministry. In turn, they expect great things from God! They also understand that God's blessings come on God's terms and not ours!

PAUL: I think you are right about this, Kim: the key to trusting God and expecting great things is letting go of control and moving from a self-serving church—a profound disregard of self-interest—to focus more energy on connecting neighbors and community to the good news.

KIM: Amen! God's surprising promise for us is that God is always there—worthy of our trust and able to do great things with us.

PAUL: When I think about the strategies of Jesus, this one is woven about as deeply into his personhood and existence as any other we discuss in this book. In one respect, this goes deeper than mere strategy. This became his essence. Jesus lived trust. He experienced fear and battled it at times, but he lived trust. No minimum salary, no family safety net, a lot of powerful people at odds with his calling! A high chance of a violent end to his life met him throughout his ministry—and not just at the end of the third year. The internal struggles that are represented in the temptation narratives, they finally all resolve in his decision to trust God.

KIM: Building trust takes integrity, competency, and caring. Jesus did all that very well!

PAUL: When the Apostle Paul says to us, looking back on his life, seeking to follow the way of Jesus, that "to live is Christ and to die is gain" (Phil. 1:21 NIV), the message is clear. First, life is all about trusting God. Second, the jury will not come in fully to vindicate us for the risks taken in the name of Christ until we are in the next life.

KIM: So where is there room for fear in that?

To summarize the gospel strategy here: it's about letting go, surrendering, giving back to God what is God's! Then it is about listening, sharing, and discovering God's desires for us and our community. And then going with God, come what may! It doesn't happen overnight. Expect church decisions that hinge on trust to take some time! Be the nonanxious presence within your fellowship!

And know, that in all things, God is with you!

Consider the ravens: They do not sow or reap, they have no storeroom or barn; yet God feeds them. And how much more valuable you are than birds! Who of you by worrying can add a single hour to your life? Since you cannot do this very little thing, why do you worry about the rest?

Consider how the lilies grow. They do not labor or spin. Yet I tell you, not even Solomon in all his splendor was dressed like one of these. If that is how God clothes the grass of the field, which is here today, and tomorrow is thrown into the fire, how much more will he clothe you, O you of little faith! And do not set your heart on what you will eat or drink; do not worry about it. For the pagan world runs after all such things, and your Father knows that you need them. But seek his kingdom, and these things will be given to you as well. (Luke 12:24-31 NIV)

Everything is possible for him who believes. (Mark 9:23 NIV)

IMPROVING YOUR ODDS: AN EPILOGUE

In this book, we have discussed ten strategies for leadership, especially appropriate for the moments in which a significant change in direction or momentum is desired in the life of a faith community. Since most established American churches are now on the back side of the plateau or declining, major shifts are needed in most places. Even the few churches that are growing do so in a fast-paced culture, in which current successful ministry approaches must morph and adapt if those churches want to have a chance at reaching the next generation of adults coming behind the ones they may have figured out.

In most cases, transformational change sets in (if at all) during the early months of a new pastoral leader. Numerical net gains might not come for two to seven years after a transformation begins. But if something significant does not shift in the first two years of a pastorate, the chances of such a shift are significantly diminished. There are outlying cases in which the shift happens later; and in almost all of these cases, it correlates with a major crisis in the life of either the leader or the community. We believe that if transformation is desired, we should do all we can to encourage it in the first year of a pastor's tenure.

We do not outline a month-by-month plan for the first year or two of a new pastoral assignment; others do: both Kennon L. Callahan (*A New Beginning for Pastors and Congregations* [San Francisco: Jossey-Bass, 1999]) and Paul Borden (*Make or Break Your Church in 365 Days* [Nashville: Abingdon Press, 2012]) offer excellent resources that lay out a list of smart things to do in the first year of a new pastoral assignment. Those resources are especially helpful if one looks behind the authors' admonitions for the larger principles and the strategic thinking that drives them. Callahan and Borden are each brilliant strategists. Enjoy their books and profit richly! But *always* look for the strategy underneath their recommendations! Look beyond what they say. Catch on to how they think!

In this book, rather than mapping out what to do literally, we have focused entirely on strategy itself—in particular, ten surprising, refreshing, disorienting moves that a leader can make to open up new possibilities for a community's future. We have drawn these strategies from the gospel itself, right out of the playbook of Jesus—who, in addition to being our Savior, ranks as one of the most brilliant community organizers of all time. And he worked with only a three-year time window to make his mark. Depending in part on the gifts of the leader and the demands of the leadership challenge, you will apply these ten strategies in varying amounts. Hopefully, we have not said so much as to encroach upon the work of the Spirit or the artfulness of the leader applied to distinct places and challenges. We have led each chapter with examples of how pastors might apply this strategy or that. You can do better, in every case, leaning into the beauty of your own giftedness and the gifts of the team God places around you!

We have written this book in lay-clergy dialogue to underline the fact that effective church leadership is always a partnership and a collaborative effort. And yet we have led each chapter with a story focused on pastoral leadership in the early moments of a new pastoral assignment, underlining the fact that strategic, artful pastoral leadership is absolutely critical.

A free group study/processing guide is available for download at www. epicentergroup.org.

Now for a sobering word: the odds are probably against you at the outset. The odds were certainly against Jesus. Why else would he keep shifting the focus from the obviously miserable odds of his movement to the truth that "with God all things are possible" (Matt. 19:26 NIV)?

For all the church transformations that occur each year, many more churches just continue on the paths they already travel. There are many reasons for this. Some places are harder than other places. Some places have complicated internal history or even untended emotional wounds from a pastoral predator years before. Some places require very thick skin and persistent faith applied over several years. Some places are very isolated from the world and community that is evolving around them. Sometimes, a change begins and the pastor or key lay leader decides to move before the transformation is mature—and things easily slide back to where they started, or worse. Sometimes, pastors are sent or called to places where they are, culturally, like fish out of water from the first day. That's tough. Sometimes, pastors are still a bit green in their own leadership development—sent to a tough challenge before they have been able to develop the array of skills necessary to tackle it. Sometimes people are entrenched in a church with a death grip on the place, and that grip is not easily loosened.

But you can change your odds. This much is clear.

So, as we close these pages, we want to leave you with some thoughts about how you can improve your odds—beyond the wisdom of Jesus' core strategies.

1. Enlist a prayer team to pray for you and your family 365 days a year. Get them organized before the moving van arrives in that new place! Draw them from all over the planet if necessary, at least a half dozen dependable, praying people. Communicate with them electronically and often. Even in new-church starts that seem filled with hope and possibility, there are traps everywhere and spiritual darkness that will push back. For some of you more liberal types, this kind of talk may creep you out. But take our word on this one. Regardless of their theology going in, most pastors who pull off either a church transformation or a new-church start end up believing in the devil or in something much more formidable and well organized than what they believed in when they graduated from seminary. And of course you know what Jesus thought about this subject. Believe what you want about the nature of evil, but we've worked with enough folks to be able to tell the stories—and weird, weird things happen when God's people decide to assail the strongholds. You want a prayer team covering your backside because you are doing dangerous work.

2. Get a coach. When you get on the ministry field, so much comes at you so fast that it is hard to keep perspective. This is true even for the most seasoned and skilled pastors. A coach can help immensely. You want someone you can talk to honestly and who can talk to you honestly, who doesn't live with you, and who doesn't supervise or evaluate you.

Now both of us coach, and both us have worked with coaches. So we are more than a little opinionated about this. Find someone with a track record or someone associated with people who have a track record. Seriously. Next, interview that person. If you don't feel the mojo, interview several. Coaching relationships do not work well unless both coach and coaching client feel a certain connection with the process. If you like, take a coaching test-drive for a month or two before signing a longer-term contract. You will pay for these sessions—and you can draw upon continuing education funds, denominational grants, or funds that could be authorized by your local church leaders. Coaching is a small investment for your church to make given the high stakes that surround your succeeding as a leader there. You may end up taking weird time slots in your coach's schedule before you become a part of the established rhythm of a coach's calendar. But you want to make sure that the relationship is helpful to you. And I would rather talk to a good coach at a weird time than a mediocre coach in the middle of my workday.

The coach is for you as a pastoral leader. You may decide to pull your coach into other relationships with your church leaders at some point, or not. But you need a place where you can say things that no other human being needs to hear.

3. Learn the people in your church. And learn some key people in your community! Get a team to help you do the logistics and scheduling to meet in small-venue conversations for face time with 200, 300, or 400 people in a few weeks' time. Set up the goals of what you are seeking to accomplish with this team. They set up meetings and you show up, fresh and ready to engage new friends. Listen more than you talk. Give people a clear clue as to what you are about, but do not lay out detailed plans in these meetings. You don't know enough yet to do that. Listen, learn, and when you get to the car after the meeting, take fifteen minutes to write down everything you can recall from the meeting. Those notes, as they accumulate, will be priceless. You will want to keep milling about the people after three months, but a blitz on the front end has almost no downsides and is just loaded with benefits.

Paul's friend who works at the White House leads a team of interns. She and they work fifteen- to eighteen-hour days. Granted they are young and ambitious folks, without kids at home, but there is only one way to keep them fired up and on mission, working that hard over an extended period of months or years: they all get regular face time with Barack Obama. Often. He is in touch with the people on his team. He gathers them in a room for a few minutes. He listens. He casts vision. He helps renew the team's commitment to the tasks before them. If the president of the United States can find time to do this, you can.

4. Preach the best you can every week. Don't cut corners on this, especially if you feel it is not your greatest gift as a pastor. It's a big rock in the bucket for every pastor, every single week. In all sized churches! First impressions are made not only on your first Sunday but almost every Sunday for someone. All of us preach differently. Be who you are, and be the best you in preaching that you can be! Whatever you have to say, allow it to grow from your fresh engagement with new ideas and with Scripture. Always step up to preach in a hopeful frame of mind. Talk about stuff that feels relevant to the person walking in for the first time. People do not come to church for the church to talk through its ministry challenges. That is a major turnoff! Do that somewhere besides worship. People need a word that challenges them personally, blesses them personally, and guides them personally to a better way of living. And the more directly you can draw the connection to the Scriptures, the more compelling your words will be for most folks.

5. Consider bringing in a ministry strategist or a strategy team for intensive consultation at some point after the first six months. Your coach may be the right person for this, or perhaps there is someone more specialized, but it has been the experience of hundreds of churches that a good strategist coming in at just the right time to talk about just the right things can save three years of wandering around in the wilderness. Especially since we know the clock is always ticking, both in terms of how long we have to stick around in a place as leader and in terms of various "windows of opportunity." Sometimes, you will schedule this person a year or more in advance. Sometimes you may work with a team of two (this is the norm with the Healthy Church Initiative in United Methodism). Sometimes, you will work with one seasoned ministry consultant.

This is a choice even more critical than a choice of coach. The coach can be replaced quietly without disruption of church life. The consultant will have much more direct impact, whether or not you buy into her or his convictions and recommendations. So shop carefully. Talk to references. Be aware that the person who was so effective in Church X (a church very different from yours) may or may not be effective in your situation. The best consultants are able to work in a wide variety of contexts, but no consultant is going to be at her or his best just anywhere. You might ask them the places that are hardest for them to work effectively and discover some helpful information.

In most cases, on-site consultation is best delayed until after a pastor has been in place at least six months. There are exceptions. If a church is mired in difficult long-term issues, if there is imminent crisis, or if aftercare is needed in the wake of church trauma, then you may decide to bring the consultant in within three months of a pastor's arrival.

6. Tend to your soul. Get a spiritual director or share in a spiritual support/accountability group. This is basic stuff for all pastors and spiritual leaders. But it is amazing how often we find people seeking to tackle enormous tasks without a sufficient spiritual support network. The local clergy cluster is most likely *not* the support you need the most.

7. Sleep, exercise, take your day off, and eat your vegetables. Seriously. And go home to play with your kids or your dog. Even in the most intense challenges, please keep a life beyond church! Swim, run, golf, bowl, play tennis, coach little league, tinker on an antique car, or cook crazy, fun food worthy of the Food Channel—and with as few of your church people as possible!

Log your comp time when you work a ridiculously long week, and reward yourself with those hours *paid back* to you and your family within a month. *You do not need to ask anyone's permission to log comp time.* You are not working the register at McDonald's. Just do good work, and quietly observe comp time, an hour here, an hour there, a half day here, and a half day there. If people ask you to do something during your comp time or during a day off, tell them, "I would love to do that, but I already have an obligation then. What about if we try for [name another time]?"

In almost every intense church transformation and new-church plant, there is a point when the leader's significant other enters the room (usually at home, and often in the evening) without a smile and says, "Sit down. We need to talk." And when that happens, you listen—you can even take notes. But when he or she is done, you say the following words (you can say them exactly as printed if you wish): "Thank you, honey. You are totally right. I have lost perspective. Please forgive me. Help me get back on track here. Let's get these changes on my calendar within the next week."

And the better you are as a change agent and kingdom mover and shaker, the more likely that this conversation will be coming soon to a living room near you. Just roll with it, and thank the Lord and all your lucky stars for a spouse who loves you enough to demand some needed changes once in a while.

8. Have fun. You are not God, and so don't take your part of God's work so seriously that you lose the playfulness. Lighten up. Laugh at the silliness you occasionally encounter. Find friends far from your church system to whom you can tell the funny stories. And at all times, celebrate the good life that God makes possible!

There is an old saying. All of us have heard it. *If Mama ain't happy, ain't nobody happy!* The same can be said of pastors.

Blessings to each of you in the holy work God has set before you!